THE CITIES OF
JAPAN

THE WORLD 100 YEARS AGO

Berlin

Egypt

The Cities of Japan

London

Moscow

Paris

Peking

Southern Italy

THE WORLD **100** YEARS AGO

BURTON HOLMES

THE CITIES OF
JAPAN

FRED L. ISRAEL
General Editor

ARTHUR M. SCHLESINGER, JR.
Senior Consulting Editor

CHELSEA HOUSE PUBLISHERS
Philadelphia

CHELSEA HOUSE PUBLISHERS

EDITOR-IN-CHIEF Stephen Reginald
MANAGING EDITOR James D. Gallagher
PRODUCTION MANAGER Pamela Loos
ART DIRECTOR Sara Davis
PICTURE EDITOR Judy Hasday
SENIOR PRODUCTION EDITOR Lisa Chippendale
ASSOCIATE ART DIRECTOR Takeshi Takahashi
COVER DESIGN Dave Loose Design

First Printing

1 3 5 7 9 8 6 4 2

Library of Congress Cataloging-in-Publication Data

Holmes, Burton, b. 1870.
The cities of Japan/ by Burton Holmes; Fred L. Israel, general editor; Arthur M. Schlesinger, jr., senior consulting editor.
 p. cm. —(The world 100 years ago)
Includes index.

ISBN 0-7910-4668-0 (hc). ISBN 0-7910-4669-9 (pb).

1. Holmes, Burton, b. 1870—Journeys—Japan. 2. Japan——Description and travel. I. Israel, Fred L. II. Schlesinger, Arthur Meier, 1917- . III. Title. IV. Series: Holmes, Burton, b. 1870. World 100 years ago today.
DS809.H74   1997
915.204'31—dc21   97-39520
                                                      CIP

CONTENTS

The Great Globe Trotter   6
Irving Wallace

Burton Holmes   24
Arthur M. Schlesinger, jr.

The World 100 Years Ago   26
Dr. Fred Israel

The Cities of Japan   35

Further Reading   132

Contributors   133

Index   134

THE GREAT GLOBE TROTTER

By Irving Wallace

One day in the year 1890, Miss Nellie Bly, of the *New York World,* came roaring into Brooklyn on a special train from San Francisco. In a successful effort to beat Phileas Fogg's fictional 80 days around the world, Miss Bly, traveling with two handbags and flannel underwear, had circled the globe in 72 days, 6 hours, and 11 minutes. Immortality awaited her.

Elsewhere that same year, another less-publicized globe-girdler made his start toward immortality. He was Mr. Burton Holmes, making his public debut with slides and anecdotes ("Through Europe With a Kodak") before the Chicago Camera Club. Mr. Holmes, while less spectacular than his feminine rival, was destined, for that very reason, soon to dethrone her as America's number-one traveler.

Today, Miss Bly and Mr. Holmes have one thing in common: In the mass mind they are legendary vagabonds relegated to the dim and dusty past of the Iron Horse and the paddle-wheel steamer. But if Miss Bly, who shuffled off this mortal coil in 1922, is now only a part of our folklore, there are millions to testify that

Mr. Burton Holmes, aged seventy-six, is still very much with us.

Remembering that Mr. Holmes was an active contemporary of Miss Bly's, that he was making a livelihood at traveling when William McKinley, John L. Sullivan, and Admiral Dewey ruled the United States, when Tony Pastor, Lily Langtry, and Lillian Russell ruled the amusement world, it is at once amazing and reassuring to pick up the daily newspapers of 1946 and find, sandwiched between advertisements of rash young men lecturing on "Inside Stalin" and "I Was Hitler's Dentist," calm announcements that tomorrow evening Mr. Burton Holmes has something more to say about "Beautiful Bali."

Burton Holmes, a brisk, immaculate, chunky man with gray Vandyke beard, erect bearing, precise speech ("folks are always mistaking me for Monty Woolley," he says, not unhappily), is one of the seven wonders of the entertainment world. As Everyman's tourist, Burton Holmes has crossed the Atlantic Ocean thirty times, the Pacific Ocean twenty times, and has gone completely around the world six times. He has spent fifty-five summers abroad, and recorded a half million feet of film of those summers. He was the first person to take motion picture cameras into Russia and Japan. He witnessed the regular decennial performance of the Passion Play at Oberammergau in 1890, and attended the first modern Olympics at Athens in 1896. He rode on the first Trans-Siberian train across Russia, and photographed the world's first airplane meet at Rheims.

As the fruit of these travels, Burton Holmes has delivered approximately 8,000 illustrated lectures that have grossed, according to an estimate by *Variety,* five million dollars in fifty-three winters. Because he does not like to be called a lecturer— "I'm a performer," he insists, "and I have performed on more legitimate stages than platforms"—he invented the word "travelogue" in London to describe his activity.

His travelogues, regarded as a fifth season of the year in most communities, have won him such popularity that he holds the record for playing in the longest one-man run in American show business. In the five and a half decades past, Burton Holmes has successively met the hectic competition of big-time vaudeville, stage, silent pictures, radio, and talking pictures, and he has survived them all.

At an age when most men have retired to slippered ease or are hounded by high blood pressure, Burton Holmes is more active and more popular than ever before. In the season just finished, which he started in San Francisco during September, 1945, and wound up in New York during April, 1946, Holmes appeared in 187 shows, a record number. He averaged six travelogues a week, spoke for two hours at each, and did 30 percent more box-office business than five years ago. Not once was a scheduled lecture postponed or canceled. In fact, he has missed only two in his life. In 1935, flying over the Dust Bowl, he suffered laryngitis and was forced to bypass two college dates. He has never canceled an appearance before a paid city audience. Seven years ago, when one of his elderly limbs was fractured in an automobile crack-up in Finland, there was a feeling that Burton Holmes might not make the rounds. When news of the accident was released, it was as if word had gone out that Santa Claus was about to cancel his winter schedule. But when the 1939 season dawned, Burton Holmes rolled on the stage in a wheelchair, and from his seat of pain (and for 129 consecutive appearances thereafter), he delivered his travel chat while 16-mm film shimmered on the screen beside him.

Today, there is little likelihood that anything, except utter extinction, could keep Holmes from his waiting audiences. Even now, between seasons, Holmes is in training for his next series— 150 illustrated lectures before groups in seventeen states.

Before World War II, accompanied by Margaret Oliver, his wife of thirty-two years, Holmes would spend his breathing spells on summery excursions through the Far East or Europe. While aides captured scenery on celluloid, Holmes wrote accom-

panying lecture material in his notebooks. Months later, he
would communicate his findings to his cult, at a maximum price
of $1.50 per seat. With the outbreak of war, Holmes changed his
pattern. He curtailed travel outside the Americas. This year,
except for one journey to Las Vegas, Nevada, where he personal-
ly photographed cowboy cutups and shapely starlets at the annual Helldorado festival, Holmes has been allowing his assistants to
do all his traveling for him.

Recently, one crew, under cameraman Thayer Soule, who
helped shoot the Battle of Tarawa for the Marines, brought
Holmes a harvest of new film from Mexico. Another crew, after
four months in Brazil last year, and two in its capital this year,
returned to Holmes with magnificent movies. Meantime, other
crews, under assignment from Holmes, are finishing films on
Death Valley, the West Indies, and the Mississippi River.

In a cottage behind his sprawling Hollywood hilltop home,
Holmes is busy, day and night, sorting the incoming negative,
cutting and editing it, and rewriting lectures that will accompany
the footage this winter. He is too busy to plan his next trip. More-
over, he doesn't feel that he should revisit Europe yet. "I wouldn't
mind seeing it," he says, "but I don't think my public would be
interested. My people want a good time, they want escape, they
want sweetness and light, beauty and charm. There is too much
rubble and misery over there now, and I'll let those picture mag-
azines and Fox Movietone newsreels show all that. I'll wait until
it's tourist time again."

When he travels, he thinks he will visit three of the four acces-
sible places on earth that he has not yet seen. One is Tahiti, which
he barely missed a dozen times, and the other two are Iran and
Iraq. The remaining country that he has not seen, and has no
wish to see, is primitive Afghanistan. Of all cities on earth, he
would most like to revisit Kyoto, once capital of Japan. He still
recalls that the first movies ever made inside Japan were ones he
made in Kyoto, in 1899. The other cities he desires to revisit are

Venice and Rome. The only island for which he has any longing is Bali—"the one quaint spot on earth where you can really get away from it all."

In preparing future subjects, Holmes carefully studies the success of his past performances. Last season, his two most popular lectures in the East were "California" and "Adventures in Mexico." The former grossed $5,100 in two Chicago shows; the latter jammed the St. Louis Civic Auditorium with thirty-five hundred potential señores and señoritas. Holmes will use these subjects again, with revisions, next season, and add some brand-new Latin American and United States topics. He will sidestep anything relating to war. He feels, for example, that anything dealing with the once exotic Pacific islands might have a questionable reception—"people will still remember those white crosses they saw in newsreels of Guadalcanal and Iwo Jima."

Every season presents its own obstacles, and the next will challenge Holmes with a new audience of travel-sated and disillusioned ex-GI's. Many of these men, and their families, now know that a South Sea island paradise means mosquitoes and malaria and not Melville's Fayaway and Loti's Rarahu. They know Europe means mud and ruins and not romance. Nevertheless, Holmes is confident that he will win these people over.

"The veterans of World War II will come to my travelogues just as their fathers did. After the First World War, I gave illustrated lectures on the sights of France, and the ex-doughboys enjoyed them immensely. But I suppose there's no use comparing that war to this. The First World War was a minor dispute between gentlemen. In this one, the atrocities and miseries will be difficult to forget. I know I can't give my Beautiful Italy lecture next season to men who know Italy only as a pigsty, but you see, in my heart Italy is forever beautiful, and I see things in Italy they can't see, poor fellows. How could they? . . . Still, memory is frail, and one day these boys will forget and come to my lectures not to hoot but to relive the better moments and enjoy themselves."

While Burton Holmes prepares his forthcoming shows, his business manager, a slightly built dynamo named Walter Everest, works on next season's bookings. Everest contacts organizations interested in sponsoring a lecture series, arranges dates and prices, and often leases auditoriums on his own. Everest concentrates on cities where Holmes is known to be popular, Standing Room Only cities like New York, Boston, Philadelphia, Chicago, Los Angeles. On the other hand, he is cautious about the cities where Holmes has been unpopular in the past—Toledo, Cleveland, Indianapolis, Cincinnati. The one city Holmes now avoids entirely is Pomona, California, where, at a scheduled Saturday matinee, he found himself facing an almost empty house. The phenomenon of a good city or a poor city is inexplicable. In rare cases, there may be a reason for failure, and then Holmes will attempt to resolve it. When San Francisco was stone-deaf to Holmes, investigation showed that he had been competing with the annual opera season. Last year, he rented a theater the week before the opera began. He appeared eight times and made a handsome profit.

Once Holmes takes to the road for his regular season, he is a perpetual-motion machine. Leaving his wife behind, he barnstorms with his manager, Everest, and a projectionist, whirling to Western dates in his Cadillac, making long hops by plane, following the heavier Eastern circuit by train. Holmes likes to amaze younger men with his activities during a typical week. If he speaks in Detroit on a Tuesday night, he will lecture in Chicago on Wednesday evening, in Milwaukee on Thursday, be back in Chicago for Friday evening and a Saturday matinee session, then go on to Kansas City on Sunday, St. Louis on Monday, and play a return engagement in Detroit on Tuesday.

This relentless merry-go-round (with Saturday nights off to attend a newsreel "and see what's happening in the world") invigorates Holmes, but grinds his colleagues to a frazzle. One morning last season, after weeks of trains and travel, Walter

Everest was awakened by a porter at six. He rose groggily, sat swaying on the edge of his berth trying to put on his shoes. He had the look of a man who had pushed through the Matto Grosso on foot. He glanced up sleepily, and there, across the aisle, was Holmes, fully dressed, looking natty and refreshed. Holmes smiled sympathetically. "I know, Walter," he said, "this life is tiring. One day both of us ought to climb on some train and get away from it all."

In his years on the road, Holmes has come to know his audience thoroughly. He is firm in the belief that it is composed mostly of traveled persons who wish to savor the glamorous sights of the world again. Through Burton, they relive their own tours. Of the others, some regard a Holmes performance as a preview. They expect to travel; they want to know the choice sights for their future three-month jaunt to Ecuador. Some few, who consider themselves travel authorities, come to a Holmes lecture to point out gleefully the good things that he missed. "It makes them happy," Holmes says cheerfully. Tomorrow's audience, for the most, will be the same as the one that heard the Master exactly a year before. Generations of audiences inherit Holmes, one from the other.

An average Holmes lecture combines the atmosphere of a revival meeting and a family get-together at which home movies are shown. A typical Holmes travelogue begins in a brightly lit auditorium, at precisely three minutes after eight-thirty. The three minutes is to allow for latecomers. Holmes, attired in formal evening clothes, strides from the wings to center stage. People applaud; some cheer. Everyone seems to know him and to know exactly what to expect. Holmes smiles broadly. He is compact, proper, handsome. His goatee dominates the scene. He has worn it every season, with the exception of one in 1895 (when, beardless, he somewhat resembled Paget's Sherlock Holmes). Now, he speaks crisply. He announces that this is the third lecture of his fifty-fourth season. He announces his subject—"Adventures in Mexico."

He walks to one side of the stage, where a microphone is standing. The lights are dimmed. The auditorium becomes dark. Beyond the fifth row, Holmes cannot be seen. The all-color 16-mm film is projected on the screen. The film opens, minus title and credits, with a shot through the windshield of an automobile speeding down the Pan-American Highway to Monterrey. Holmes himself is the sound track. His speech, with just the hint of a theatrical accent, is intimate, as if he were talking in a living room. He punctuates descriptive passages with little formal jokes. When flowers and orange trees of Mexico are on the screen, he says, "We have movies and talkies, but now we should have smellies and tasties"—and he chuckles.

The film that he verbally captions is a dazzling, uncritical montage of Things Mexican. There is a señora selling tortillas, and close-ups of how tortillas are made. There is a bullfight, but not the kill. There is snow-capped Popocatepetl, now for sale at the bargain price of fifteen million dollars. There are the pyramids outside Mexico City, older than those of Egypt, built by the ancient Toltecs who went to war with wooden swords so that they would not kill their enemies.

Holmes's movies and lectures last two hours, with one intermission. The emphasis is on description, information, and oddity. Two potential ingredients are studiously omitted. One is adventure, the other politics. Holmes is never spectacular. "I want nothing dangerous. I don't care to emulate the explorers, to risk my neck, to be the only one or the first one there. Let others tackle the Himalayas, the Amazon, the North Pole, let them break the trails for me. I'm just a Cook's tourist, a little ahead of the crowd, but not too far ahead." Some years ago, Holmes did think that he was an explorer, and became very excited about it, he now admits sheepishly. This occurred in a trackless sector of Northern Rhodesia. Holmes felt that he had discovered a site never before seen by an outsider. Grandly, he planted the flag of the Explorers

Club, carefully he set up his camera, and then, as he prepared to shoot, his glance fell upon an object several feet away—an empty Kodak carton. Quietly, he repacked and stole away—and has stayed firmly on the beaten paths ever since.

As to politics, it never taints his lectures. He insists neither he nor his audiences are interested. "When you discuss politics," he says, "you are sure to offend." Even after his third trip to Russia, he refused to discuss politics. "I am a traveler," he explained at that time, "and not a student of political and economic questions. To me, Communism is merely one of the sights I went to see."

However, friends know that Holmes has his pet panacea for the ills of the world. He is violent about the gold standard, insisting that it alone can make all the world prosperous. Occasionally, when the mood is on him, and against his better judgment, he will inject propaganda in favor of the gold standard into an otherwise timid travelogue.

When he is feeling mellow, Holmes will confess that once in the past he permitted politics to intrude upon his sterile chitchat. It was two decades ago, when he jousted with Prohibition. While not a dedicated drinking man, Holmes has been on a friendly basis with firewater since the age of sixteen. In the ensuing years, he has regularly, every dusk before dinner, mixed himself one or two highballs. Only once did he try more than two, and the results were disastrous. "Any man who drinks three will drink three hundred," he now says righteously. Holmes felt that Prohibition was an insult to civilized living. As a consequence of this belief, his audiences during the days of the Eighteenth Amendment were often startled to hear Holmes extol the virtues of open drinking, in the middle of a placid discourse on Oberammergau or Lapland. "Sometimes an indignant female would return her tickets to the rest of my series," he says, "but there were others, more intelligent, to take her place."

This independent attitude in Holmes was solely the product of his personal success. Born in January, 1870, of a financially secure, completely cosmopolitan Chicago family, he was able to be independent from his earliest days. His father, an employee in the Third National Bank, distinguished himself largely by lending George Pullman enough cash to transform his old day coaches into the first Pullman Palace Sleeping Cars, and by refusing a half interest in the business in exchange for his help. Even to this day, it makes Burton Holmes dizzy to think of the money he might have saved in charges for Pullman berths.

Holmes's interest in show business began at the age of nine when his grandmother, Ann W. Burton, took him to hear John L. Stoddard lecture on the Passion Play at Oberammergau. Young Holmes was never the same again. After brief visits to faraway Florida and California, he quit school and accompanied his grandmother on his first trip abroad. He was sixteen and wide-eyed. His grandmother, who had traveled with her wine-salesman husband to France and Egypt and down the Volga in the sixties, was the perfect guide. But this journey through Europe was eclipsed, four years later, by a more important pilgrimage with his grandmother to Germany. The first day at his hotel in Munich, Holmes saw John L. Stoddard pass through the lobby reading a Baedeker. He was petrified. It was as if he had seen his Maker. Even now, over a half century later, when Holmes speaks about Stoddard, his voice carries a tinge of awe. For eighteen years of the later nineteenth century, Stoddard, with black-and-white slides and magnificent oratory, dominated the travel-lecture field. To audiences, young and old, he was the most romantic figure in America. Later, at Oberammergau, Holmes sat next to Stoddard through the fifteen acts of the Passion Play and they became friends.

When Holmes returned to the States, some months after Nellie Bly had made her own triumphal return to Brooklyn, he showed rare Kodak negatives of his travels to fellow members of the Chicago Camera Club. The members were impressed, and one suggested that these be mounted as slides and shown to the general public. "To take the edge off the silence, to keep the show moving," says Holmes, "I wrote an account of my journey and read it, as the stereopticon man changed slides." The show, which grossed the club $350, was Holmes's initial travelogue. However, he dates the beginning of his professional career from three years later, when he appeared under his own auspices with hand-colored slides.

After the Camera Club debut, Holmes did not go immediately into the travelogue field. He was not yet ready to appreciate its possibilities. Instead, he attempted to sell real estate, and failed. Then he worked for eight dollars a week as a photo supply clerk. In 1902, aching with wanderlust, he bullied his family into staking him to a five-month tour of Japan. On the boat he was thrilled to find John L. Stoddard, also bound for Japan. They became closer friends, even though they saw Nippon through different eyes. "The older man found Japan queer, quaint, comfortless, and almost repellent," Stoddard's son wrote years later. "To the younger man it was a fairyland." Stoddard invited Holmes to continue on around the world with him, but Holmes loved Japan and decided to remain.

When Holmes returned to Chicago, the World's Columbian Exposition of 1893 was in full swing. He spent months at the Jackson Park grounds, under Edison's new electric lights, listening to Lillian Russell sing, Susan B. Anthony speak, and watching Sandow perform feats of strength. With rising excitement, he observed Jim Brady eating, Anthony Comstock snorting at Little Egypt's hootchy-kootchy, and Alexander Dowie announcing himself as the Prophet Elijah III.

In the midst of this excitement came the depression of that year. Holmes's father suffered. "He hit the wheat pit at the wrong time, and I had to go out on my own," says Holmes. "The photo supply house offered me fifteen dollars a week to return. But I didn't want to work. The trip to Japan, the Oriental exhibits of the Exposition, were still on my mind. I thought of

Stoddard. I thought of the slides I'd had hand-colored in Tokyo. That was it, and it wasn't work. So I hired a hall and became a travel lecturer."

Copying society addresses from his mother's visiting list, and additional addresses from *The Blue Book,* Holmes mailed two thousand invitations in the form of Japanese poem-cards. Recipients were invited to two illustrated lectures, at $1.50 each, on "Japan—the Country and the Cities." Both performances were sellouts. Holmes grossed $700.

For four years Holmes continued his fight to win a steady following, but with only erratic success. Then, in 1897, when he stood at the brink of defeat, two events occurred to change his life. First, John L. Stoddard retired from the travel-lecture field and threw the platforms of the nation open to a successor. Second, Holmes supplemented colored slides with a new method of illustrating his talks. As his circular announced, "There will be presented for the first time in connection with a course of travel lectures a series of pictures to which a modern miracle has added the illusion of life itself—the reproduction of recorded motion."

Armed with his jumpy movies—scenes of the Omaha fire department, a police parade in Chicago, Italians eating spaghetti, each reel running twenty-five seconds, with a four-minute wait between reels—Burton Holmes invaded the Stoddard strongholds in the East. Stoddard came to hear him and observe the newfangled movies. Like Marshal Foch who regarded the airplane as "an impractical toy," Stoddard saw no future in the motion picture. Nevertheless, he gave young Holmes a hand by insisting that Augustin Daly lease his Manhattan theater to the newcomer. This done, Stoddard retired to the Austrian Tyrol, and Holmes went on to absorb Stoddard's audiences in Boston and Philadelphia and to win new followers of his own throughout the nation.

His success assured, Holmes began to gather material with a vigor that was to make him one of history's most indefatigable travelers. In 1900, at the Paris Exposition, sitting in a restaurant built like a Russian train, drinking vodka while a colored panorama of Siberia rolled past his window, he succumbed to this unique advertising of the new Trans-Siberian railway and bought a ticket. The trip in 1901 was a nightmare. After ten days on the Trans Siberian train, which banged along at eleven miles an hour, Holmes was dumped into a construction train for five days, and then spent twenty-seven days on steamers going down the Amur River. It took him forty-two and a half days to travel from Moscow to Vladivostok.

But during that tour, he had one great moment. He saw Count Leo Tolstoi at Yasnaya Polyana, the author's country estate near Tula. At a dinner in Moscow, Holmes met Albert J. Beveridge, the handsome senator from Indiana. Beveridge had a letter of introduction to Tolstoi and invited Holmes and his enormous 60-mm movie camera to come along. Arriving in a four-horse landau, the Americans were surprised to find Tolstoi's house dilapidated. Then, they were kept waiting two hours. At last, the seventy-three-year-old, white-bearded Tolstoi, nine years away from his lonely death in a railway depot, appeared. He was attired in a mujik costume. He invited his visitors to breakfast, then conversed in fluent English. "He had only a slight accent, and he spoke with the cadence of Sir Henry Irving," Holmes recalls.

Of the entire morning's conversation, Holmes remembers clearly only one remark. That was when Tolstoi harangued, "There should be no law. No man should have the right to judge or condemn another. Absolute freedom of the individual is the only thing that can redeem the world. Christ was a great teacher, nothing more!" As Tolstoi continued to speak, Holmes quietly set up his movie camera. Tolstoi had never seen one before. He posed stiffly, as for a daguerreotype. When he thought that it was over, and resumed his talking, Holmes began actual shooting. This priceless film never reached the screen. Senator Beveridge was then a presidential possibility. His managers feared that this film of Beveridge with a Russian radical might be used by his opponents. The film was taken from Holmes and destroyed. Later, when he was not even nominated for the presidency, Beveridge wrote an apology to Holmes, "for this destruction of so valuable a living record of the grand old Russian."

In 1934, at a cost of ten dollars a day, Holmes spent twenty-one days in modern Soviet Russia. He loved the ballet, the omelets, the Russian rule against tipping, and the lack of holdups. He went twice to see the embalmed Lenin, fascinated by the sight of "his head resting on a red pillow like that of a tired man asleep."

Although Holmes's name had already appeared on eighteen travel volumes, this last Russian trip inspired him to write his first and only original book. The earlier eighteen volumes, all heavily illustrated, were offered as a set, of which over forty thousand were sold. However, they were not "written," but were actually a collection of lectures delivered orally by Holmes. The one book that he wrote as a book, *The Traveler's Russia,* published in 1934 by G.P. Putnam's Sons, was a failure. Holmes has bought the remainders and passes them out to guests with a variety of inscriptions. In a serious mood he will inscribe, "To travel is to possess the world." In a frivolous mood, he will write "With love from Tovarich Burtonovitch Holmeski."

In the five decades past, Holmes has kept himself occupied with a wide variety of pleasures, such as attending Queen Victoria's Golden Jubilee in London, chatting with Admiral Dewey in Hong Kong, driving the first automobile seen in Denmark, and photographing a mighty eruption of Vesuvius.

In 1918, wearing a war correspondent's uniform, he shot army scenes on the Western Front and his films surpassed those of the poorly organized newsreel cameramen. In 1923, flying for the first time, he had his most dangerous experience, when his plane almost crashed between Toulouse and Rabat. Later, in

Berlin, he found his dollar worth ten million marks, and in Africa he interviewed Emperor Haile Selassie in French, and, closer to home, he flew 20,000 miles over Central and South America.

Burton Holmes enjoys company on his trips. By coincidence, they are often celebrities. Holmes traveled through Austria with Maria Jeritza, through Greece with E.F. Benson, through the Philippines with Dr. Victor Heiser. He covered World War I with Harry Franck, wandered about Japan with Lafcadio Hearn's son, crossed Ethiopia with the Duke of Gloucester. He saw Hollywood with Mary Pickford, Red Square with Alma Gluck, and the Andes with John McCutcheon.

Of the hundreds of travelogues that Holmes has delivered, the most popular was "The Panama Canal." He offered this in 1912, when the "big ditch" was under construction, and news-hungry citizens flocked to hear him. Among less timely subjects, his most popular was the standard masterpiece on Oberammergau, followed closely by his illustrated lectures on the "Frivolities of Paris," the "Canals of Venice," the "Countryside of England" and, more currently, "Adventures in Mexico." Burton Holmes admits that his greatest failure was an elaborate travelogue on Siam, even though it seemed to have everything except Anna and the King thereof. Other failures included travelogues on India, Burma, Ethiopia, and—curiously—exotic Bali. The only two domestic subjects to fizzle were "Down in Dixie" in 1915 and "The Century of Progress Exposition" in 1932.

All in all, the success of Holmes's subjects has been so consistently high that he has never suffered seriously from competition. One rival died, another retired eight years ago. "I'm the lone survivor of the magic-lantern boys," says Holmes. Of the younger crowd, Holmes thought that Richard Halliburton might become his successor. "He deserved to carry the banner," says Holmes. "He was good-looking, with a fine classical background, intelligent, interesting, and he really did those darn-fool stunts." Halliburton, who had climbed the Matterhorn, swum the Hellespont, followed the Cortés train through Mexico, lectured with slides. "I told him to throw away the slides," says Holmes. "He was better without them, his speech was so colorful." When Halliburton died attempting to sail a Chinese junk across the Pacific, Holmes decided to present an illustrated lecture on "The Romantic Adventures of Richard Halliburton." He used his own movies but, in the accompanying talk, Halliburton's written text. "It was a crashing failure," sighs Holmes. "His millions of fans did not want to hear me, and my fans did not want to know about him."

For a while, Hollywood appeared to be the travelogue's greatest threat. Holmes defeated this menace by marriage with the studios. He signed a contract with Paramount, made fifty-two travel shorts each year, between 1915 and 1921. Then, with the advent of talking pictures, Holmes joined Metro-Goldwyn-Mayer and made a series of travelogues, released in English, French, Italian, Spanish. In 1933, he made his debut in radio, and in 1944 made his first appearance on television.

Today, safe in the knowledge that he is an institution, Holmes spends more and more time in his rambling, plantation-style, wooden home, called "Topside," located on a hill a mile above crowded Hollywood Boulevard. This dozen-roomed brown house, once a riding club for silent day film stars, and owned for six years by Francis X. Bushman (who gave it Hollywood's first swimming pool, where Holmes now permits neighborhood children to splash), was purchased by Holmes in 1930. "I had that M-G-M contract," he says, "and it earned me a couple of hundred thousand dollars. Well, everyone with a studio contract immediately gets himself a big car, a big house, and a small blonde. I acquired the car, the house, but kept the blonde a mental acquisition." For years, Holmes also owned a Manhattan duplex decorated with costly Japanese and Buddhist treasures, which he called "Nirvana." Before Pearl Harbor, Holmes sold the duplex, with its two-million-dollar collection of furnishings, to Robert Ripley, the cartoonist and oddity hunter.

Now, in his rare moments of leisure, Holmes likes to sit on the veranda of his Hollywood home and chat with his wife. Before he met her, he had been involved in one public romance. Gossips, everywhere, insisted that he might marry the fabulous Elsie de Wolfe, actress, millionaire decorator, friend of Oscar Wilde and Sarah Bernhardt, who later became Lady Mendl. Once, in Denver, Holmes recalls, a reporter asked him if he was engaged to Elsie de Wolfe. Holmes replied, curtly, No. That afternoon a banner headline proclaimed: BURTON HOLMES REFUSES TO MARRY ELSIE DE WOLFE!

Shortly afterward, during a photographic excursion, Holmes met Margaret Oliver who, suffering from deafness, had taken up still photography as an avocation. In 1914, following a moonlight proposal on a steamer's deck, he married Miss Oliver in New York City's St. Stephen's Episcopal Church, and took her to prosaic Atlantic City for the first few days of their honeymoon, then immediately embarked on a long trip abroad.

When his wife is out shopping, Holmes will stroll about his estate, study his fifty-four towering palm trees, return to the veranda for a highball, thumb through the *National Geographic,* play with his cats, or pick up a language textbook. He is on speaking terms with eight languages, including some of the Scandinavian, and is eager to learn more. He never reads travel books. "As Pierre Loti once remarked, 'I don't read. It might ruin my style,'" he explains.

He likes visitors, and he will startle them with allusions to his earlier contemporaries. "This lawn part reminds me of the one at which I met Emperor Meiji," he will say. Meiji, grandfather of Hirohito, opened Japan to Commodore Perry. When visitors ask for his travel advice, Holmes invariably tells them to see the Americas first. "Why go to Mont St. Michel?" he asks. "Have you seen Monticello?"

But when alone with his wife and co-workers on the veranda,

and the pressure of the new season is weeks away, he will loosen his blue dressing gown, inhale, then stare reflectively out over the sun-bathed city below.

"You know, this is the best," he will say softly, "looking down on this Los Angeles. It is heaven. I could sit here the rest of my life." Then, suddenly, he will add, "There is so much else to see and do. If only I could have another threescore years upon this planet. If only I could know the good earth better than I do."

————————

Note: Irving Wallace (1916-1990) wrote this article on the occasion of Burton Holmes's 77th birthday. It was originally printed in *The Saturday Evening Post* May 10, 1947. Holmes retired the following year from presenting his travelogues in person. He died in 1958 at age 88. His autobiography, *The World is Mine,* was published in 1953.

Reprinted by permission of Mrs. Sylvia Wallace.

Burton Holmes

By Arthur M. Schlesinger, jr.

B urton Holmes!—forgotten today, but such a familiar name in America in the first half of the 20th century, a name then almost synonymous with dreams of foreign travel. In the era before television brought the big world into the households of America, it was Burton Holmes who brought the world to millions of Americans in crowded lecture halls, and did so indefatigably for 60 years. I still remember going with my mother in the 1920s to Symphony Hall in Boston, watching the brisk, compact man with a Vandyke beard show his films of Venice or Bali or Kyoto and describe foreign lands in engaging and affectionate commentary.

Burton Holmes invented the word "travelogue" in 1904. He embodied it for the rest of his life. He was born in Chicago in 1870 and made his first trip abroad at the age of 16. Taking a camera along on his second trip, he mounted his black-and-white negatives on slides and showed them to friends in the Chicago Camera Club. "To keep the show moving," he said later, "I wrote an account of my journey and read it, as the stereopticon man changed slides." He had discovered his métier. Soon he had his slides hand-colored and was in business as a professional lecturer. In time, as technology developed, slides gave way to moving pictures.

Holmes was a tireless traveler, forever ebullient and optimistic, uninterested in politics and poverty and the darker side of life, in love with beautiful scenery, historic monuments, picturesque customs, and challenging trips. He was there at the Athens Olympics in 1896, at the opening of the Trans-Siberian railway, at the Passion Play in Oberammergau. His popular lectures had such titles as "The Magic of Mexico," "The Canals of Venice," "The Glories and Frivolities of Paris." His illustrated travel books enthralled thousands of American families. He also filmed a series of travelogues—silent pictures for Paramount, talkies for Metro-Goldwyn-Mayer.

He wanted his fellow countrymen to rejoice in the wonders of the great globe. "I'm a Cook's tourist," he said, referring to the famous tours conducted by Thomas Cook and Sons, "reporting how pleasant it is in such and such a place." He knew that the world was less than perfect, but he thought the worst sufficiently documented, and his mission, as he saw it, was to bring people the best. Reflecting at the end of the Second World War on the mood of returning veterans, he said, "The atrocities and miseries will be difficult to forget. I know I can't give my Beautiful Italy lecture next session to men who know Italy only as a pigsty . . . One day these boys will forget and come to my lectures not to hoot but to relive the better moments and enjoy themselves."

When he retired in 1951, Burton Holmes had delivered over 8,000 lectures. By the time he died in 1958, television had taken over the job he had discharged so ardently for more than half a century. He taught generations of Americans about the great world beyond the seas. His books are still readable today and show new generations how their grandparents learned about a world that has since passed away but remains a fragrant memory.

THE WORLD 100 YEARS AGO

By Dr. Fred Israel

The generation that lived 100 years ago was the first to leave behind a comprehensive visual record. It was the camera that made this possible. The great photographers of the 1860s and 1870s took their unwieldy equipment to once-unimaginable places—from the backstreets of London to the homesteads of the American frontier; from tribal Africa to the temples of Japan. They photographed almost the entire world.

Burton Holmes (1870-1958) ranks among the pioneers who popularized photojournalism. He had an insatiable curiosity. "There was for me the fascination of magic in photography," Holmes wrote. "The word Kodak had not yet been coined. You could not press the button and let someone else do the rest. You had to do it all yourself and know what you were doing." Holmes combined his love of photography with a passion for travel. It didn't really matter where—only that it be exciting.

"Shut your eyes, tight!" said Holmes. "Imagine the sands of the Sahara, the temples of Japan, the beach at Waikiki, the fjords of Norway, the vastness of Panama, the great gates of Peking." It was this type of visual imagination that made Burton Holmes America's best known travel lecturer. By his 75th birthday, he had crossed the Atlantic Ocean 30 times and the Pacific 20, and he had gone around the world on six occasions. Variety magazine estimated that in his five-decade career, Holmes had delivered more than 8,000 lectures describing almost every corner of the earth.

Burton Holmes was born in Chicago on January 8, 1870. His privileged background contributed to his lifelong fascination with travel. When he was 16, his maternal grandmother took him on a three-month European trip, about which he later wrote:

> I still recall our first meal ashore, the delicious English sole served at the Adelphi Hotel [Liverpool] . . . Edinburgh thrilled me, but Paris! I would gladly have travelled third class or on a bike or on foot. Paris at last! I knew my Paris in advance. Had I not studied the maps and plans? I knew I could find my way to Notre Dame and to the Invalides without asking anyone which way to go. (The Eiffel Tower had not yet been built.) From a bus-top, I surveyed the boulevards—recognizing all the famous sights. Then for a panoramic survey of the city, I climbed the towers of Notre Dame, then the Tour St. Jacques, the Bastille Column, and finally the Arc De Triomphe, all in one long day. That evening, I was in Montmartre, where as yet there stood no great domed church of the Sacre Coeur. But at the base of the famous hill were the red windmill wings of the Moulin Rouge revolving in all their majesty. My French—school French—was pretty bad but it sufficed. Paris was the springtime of my life!

Holmes never lost his passion for travel nor his passion for capturing his observations on film. He has left us with a unique and remarkable record that helps us to visualize the world many decades ago.

Lecturing became Holmes's profession. In 1892-93 he toured Japan. He discovered that "it was my native land in some previous incarnation—and the most beautiful land I have known." Holmes had the idea of giving an illustrated lecture about Japan to an affluent Chicago audience:

> I had brought home a large number of Japanese cards such as
> are used in Japan for sending poems or New Year's greetings.
> They were about two inches by fourteen inches long. I had the
> idea that they would, by their odd shape, attract instant notice.
> So I had envelopes made for them, employing a Japanese artist
> to make a design.

Holmes sent about 2,000 invitations to the socially prominent
whose addresses he took from the *Blue Book*. He "invited" them
to two illustrated lectures at $1.50 each on "Japan—the Country
and the Cities." ($1.50 was a high sum for the 1890s considering
that the average worker earned about $1 per day.) Both perfor-
mances sold out.

Burton Holmes's "Travelogues" (he began using the term in
1904) rapidly became part of American upper class societal life.
Holmes engaged the best theater or concert hall for a week at a
time. His appearance was an annual event at Carnegie Hall in
New York, Symphony Hall in Boston, and Orchestra Hall in
Chicago. His uncanny instinct for exciting programs invariably
received rave reviews. Once he explained how he selected his
photographic subjects:

> If I am walking through Brussels and see a dog cart or some
> other unimportant thing that is interesting enough for me to
> watch it, I am totally certain others would be interested in seeing
> a photograph of it.

A conservative man, Holmes avoided political upheavals,
economic exploitation, and social conflicts in his travelogues.
"When you discuss politics," he said, "you are sure to offend."
Holmes focused on people, places, and customs. He offered his
audience a world which was unfailingly tranquil and beautiful.

In 1897, Holmes introduced motion picture segments into his
programs. ("Neapolitans Eating Spaghetti" was his first film
clip.) His engaging personality contributed to his success. His

crisp narrative was delivered in a pleasant and cultured tone. He always wore formal dress with striped pants before an audience. Holmes took pride in creating an atmosphere so that his listeners could imagine the "Magic of Mexico" or the "Frivolities of Paris." "My first ambition was to be a magician," he said. "And, I never departed from creating illusions. I have tried to create the illusion that we are going on a journey. By projecting the views, I tried to create the illusion we are looking through 'the window of travel' upon shifting scenes." Holmes's travelogues were immensely successful financially—and Holmes became one of history's most indefatigable travelers.

Holmes's lectures took place during the winter months between the 1890s and his retirement in the early 1950s. In between, he traveled—he crossed Morocco on horseback from oasis to oasis (1894); he was in the Philippines during the 1899 insurrection; in 1901, he traversed the Russian Empire, going from Moscow to Vladivostok in 43 days. He visited Yellowstone National Park (1896) before it had been fully mapped. He was always on the move, traveling to: Venice (1896); London (1897); Hawaii (1898); The Philippines (1899); Paris (1900); Russia, China, and Korea (1901-02); Madeira, Lisbon, Denmark, and Sweden (1902); Arizona, California, and Alaska (1903); Switzerland (1904); Russia and Japan (1905); Italy, Greece, Egypt, and Hong Kong (1906); Paris, Vienna, and Germany (1907); Japan (1908); Norway (1909); Germany and Austria (1910); Brazil, Argentina, and Peru (1911); Havana and Panama (1912); India and Burma (1913); the British Isles (1914); San Francisco (1915); Canada (1916); Australia and New Zealand (1917); Belgium and Germany (1919); Turkey and the Near East (1920); England (1921); China (1922); North Africa (1923); Italy (1924); Ceylon (1925); Holland (1926); France (1927); Spain (1928); London (1929); Ethiopia (1930); California (1931); Java (1932); Chicago (1933); the Soviet Union (1934); Normandy and Brittany (1935); South America (1936); South Africa (1937); Germany (1938).

Holmes's black and white photographs have extraordinary clarity. His sharp eye for the unusual ranks him as a truly outstanding photographer and chronicler of the world.

Holmes's lectures on the Panama Canal were his most popular—cities added extra sessions. For Holmes though, his favorite presentation was always Paris—"no city charms and fascinates us like the city by the Seine." He found Athens in the morning to be the most beautiful scene in the world—"with its pearl lights and purple-blue shadows and the Acropolis rising in mystic grandeur." Above all though, Japan remained his favorite land— "one can peel away layer after layer of the serene contentment which we mistake for expressionlessness and find new beauties and surprises beneath each." And Kyoto, once the capital, was the place he wanted most to revisit—and revisit. Holmes never completed a travelogue of New York City—"I am saving the biggest thing in the world for the last." At the time of his death in 1958 at age 88, Holmes had visited most of the world. He repeatedly told interviewers that he had lived an exciting and fulfilling life because he had accomplished his goal—to travel.

In a time before television, Burton Holmes was for many people "The Travelogue Man." He brought the glamour and excitement of foreign lands to Americans unable to go themselves. His successful career spanned the years from the Spanish-American War in 1898 to the Cold War of the 1950s—a period when Americans were increasingly curious about distant places and peoples. During this time period, travel was confined to a comparative handful of the privileged. Holmes published travelogues explaining foreign cultures and customs to the masses.

In this series of splendid travel accounts, Holmes unfolds before our eyes the beauties of foreign lands as they appeared almost a century ago. These volumes contain hundreds of photographs taken by Holmes. Through his narratives and illustrations we are transported in spirit to the most interesting countries and cities of the world.

THE CITIES OF JAPAN

Burton Holmes visited Japan in 1892 and again in 1908. This travelogue explains through text and photographs what he observed—the cities, the people, and their customs.

The arrival of Commodore Matthew Perry's U.S. naval armada in 1853 was a major turning point in the history of Japan. Other Western powers followed the United States' lead in bringing the Japanese policy of economic isolation to an end. The Tokugawa regime (1600-1867) had failed to prepare Japan for the challenge from the West. In 1867, the last Tokugawa shogun (a shogun was a hereditary ruler who shared power with the Emperor) resigned, and power reverted to Emperor Meiji.

In 1868, the Emperor moved the seat of imperial power from Kyoto to Edo, renaming it Tokyo. Rapid changes and industrialization followed. This policy enabled Japan to win major military victories over China (1894-95) and Russia (1904-05).

As Holmes explains, changes were taking place throughout Japan, especially in the cities. Tokyo's new industries brought job seekers from around the country, causing the population of the city to increase rapidly. Western-style buildings were constructed in fashionable areas such as Ginza. In the 1880s, electric lighting and mass transportation were introduced. This was a period when Japan instituted compulsory primary education and developed a secondary and higher education system to rival that of Europe and the United States. Japan constructed railways, a telegraph system, and a large merchant marine. Most of the upper classes adopted Western dress.

Holmes describes a Tokyo that exists no more. On September 1, 1923, a great earthquake destroyed the city. The subsequent fires lasted several days, and more than 120,000 people were killed. Reconstruction of a new city began almost immediately.

Holmes describes Japan's cities and people at a time period

approximately halfway between the Meiji restoration (1867) and the Great Earthquake (1923). The changes that occurred during this time were truly breathtaking. Yet the new Japan that was emerging retained its traditional spirit as well as its basic institutions and customs. It is this Japan that Holmes visited. He gives us a remarkable description of a vibrant people torn between their past and the allure of Western practices.

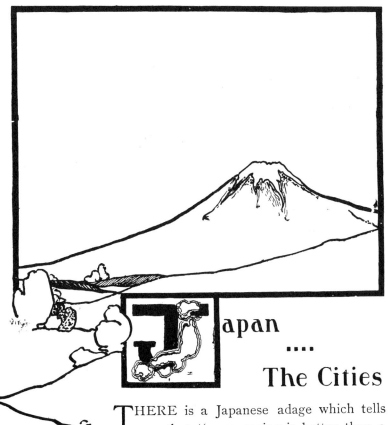

Japan ....
The Cities

THERE is a Japanese adage which tells us, that "once seeing is better than a hundred times telling about." This applies so aptly to Japan itself that it were presumptuous to attempt to give in two brief *tellings* any idea of the fascinations of the Land of the Rising Sun. But with the aid of pictures that reveal a little of the beauty of the land, it may be that these "tellings" about the country and the cities of Dai Nippon are at least better than no tale at all.

Tokyo is the greatest of Japanese cities, the metropolis and the capital of the Empire. More than a million and a half of people live in this broad, flat city, and yet there are few wide streets, and the average height of houses is only one

Photograph by Enami

TOKYO

story and a half. Tokyo viewed from an elevation looks like a cold gray choppy sea, repellent and unpromising, but there are many charming things beneath that surface of tiled roofs.

The foreign visitor is usually taken to the Imperial Hotel. Where should American and European travelers lodge if not in that magnificent establishment, where all the comforts of the Occident are provided, thanks to a thoughtful government which is determined that the stranger shall not find the greatest city of Japan deficient in hotel-accommodations of the most modern type? If you seek nothing but comfort and convenience, by all means go to the Imperial Hotel; but if, like me, you want to *feel* that you are really in Japan, pass by this splendid pile and follow me, across broad spaces, skirting the Imperial Castle, the home of the Mikado, toward a remote and thoroughly Japanese quarter of Tokyo where there are no reminders of the modern lands across the sea.

I came to Tokyo in company with a gentleman of Yokohama, a traveled Japanese, whom I had met upon a trans-Pacific steamer. He and his wife had planned a Sunday holiday in the metropolis, inviting me to meet them on the evening-train. We arrived at Shimbashi Station an hour after dark. Thence in jinrikishas we speed away through narrow streets, dark and silent, then along broad brilliant avenues, and over dozens of little bridges. This continues for an hour. Then we cross a great bridge spanning the broad Sumida River, and for half an hour dash along a smooth road on the river bank, racing up-stream with the moonbeams on the water.

"Where are you taking me?" I ask my Oriental friend, and the jinrikishas rattle so I cannot hear the answer. But presently it dawns upon me where I am. There on the other shore I see the tower, temple, and pagoda of Asakusa. This,

THE IMPERIAL HOTEL

therefore, must be Mukojima,
the famous avenue of
cherry-trees, and the
black branches
which cut grace-
ful, gloomy sil-
houettes against
the sky are the
same that we
have often seen
in pictures, glori-
ous in their spring-
time dress of pink. Yes,
we are on our way to the
far end of the long Mukojima

THE SUMIDA R
Photograph by Tamamui

highway, at least six miles from town, where we shall find an
inn that is completely and entirely Japanese in structure and
surroundings. It is called the "Yao Matsu," "The Place of
the Eight Hundred Pine-Trees." It is the most aristocratic
suburban resort of Tokyo, patronized only by the richer Japanese, unknown to foreigners, unmentioned in "Murray's,"
remote from tramways, far above the terminus of the puffy

BY THE SUMIDA RIVER

tugboats on the
river,—in a word,
secure from all the
influences which
are dispelling the
peaceful atmos-
phere and ruining
the picturesque-
ness of Japan.

Although my
friend had written
in advance for

rooms, he was not certain that we could obtain them, for the proprietor had replied to his first letter, saying : "Please do not bring the foreign gentleman of whom you speak ; we have no chairs for him to sit on, there are no beds for him to sleep in ; our chef cannot cook beefsteak ; we cannot make him comfortable." A second letter to the host assured him that the foreigner would demand no more than any native guest ; that he, in fact, preferred to be as Japanese as possible.

THE JAPANESE METROPOLIS

The unfailing courtesy of the people of this land lent an air of cordiality to our welcome at the Yao Matsu, where we arrived at half-past nine at night. It proved an ideal place, this "Place of the Eight Hundred Pine-Trees." A dozen semidetached dainty dwellings are ranged between the river and this little lake. We are very tired, very hungry, for we have not dined. Of course we shed our shoes before we enter.

IN A JAPANESE GARDEN

Mr. Sugawa and his wife—for my friends must no longer be anonymous—are dressed in Japanese kimonos, and I have not been long arrived before I, too, am just as comfortably, as coolly clad as they. Tea is served in tiny cups. Supper is ordered. Geisha are sent for to sing and play and dance for us, and all the waiting-maids, the nesan, come to take a peep at the first foreign guest the inn has ever entertained ;— but they are disappointed. I do not appear sufficiently exotic, for in my present garb I am not obtrusively American. I even sit in that conventional Japanese attitude

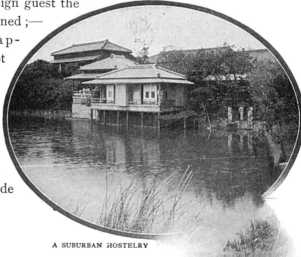

A SUBURBAN HOSTELRY

THE EVENING MEAL

which, although so try-
ing to the Occidental
knee, is assumed and held with ease and comfort by all the
other people at our supper-party. Mrs. Sugawa would never
think of sitting down in any other way; her husband, however, when at home or dining with his friends, might possibly
sit cross-legged for a little while, but never at a formal func-
tion. The Geisha, when in attendance at dinners or big ban-
quets, pass hours sitting thus, playing and singing. As for the
servants, they never come into our presence without dropping
to the floor, touching foreheads to the mats, and then sitting
back upon their heels to receive our august commands.

One nesan on the left was fearful of the flashlight, by
means of which the evening scene was photographed. Would
that I, too, had been fearful of it! The charge exploded,
almost in my right hand, and a few seconds later this little
group of new acquaintances was turned into a helpful band
of sympathetic friends. It was almost worth while to have

one's hand all but withered by that incan-
descent magnesium powder, for the
accident brought out so much of un-
suspected kindliness and solicitude.
Everybody in the house sat up with
me for three long painful hours,
until a doctor could be brought from
Tokyo.   He declares that my right
hand will be useless for a month.
And to think that I have just learned
to eat with chop-sticks and must now
begin all over, and educate the fingers of
the other hand !   But hunger is a splendid
teacher ; the awkward fingers soon pick up the knack ; in
fact, for a one-handed man, Japanese table-customs are
happily adapted.   There are no knives and forks demanding
two trained hands, and sometimes superhuman strength ; the
carving — even
the cutting up, is
done before the
food is served.

My friends left
on the following
day, and my first
thought was that
although I was to
stay in Tokyo I
should have to
move to the Im-
perial Hotel, in
other words, re-
turn to modern
civilization. But
how, on second

BREAKFAST

thought, could a disabled traveler be more advantageously situated than here in the little inn, which grows prettier every time it is looked at from a different point of view? Here are servants ever ready to put on your shoes, button your coat, insert your cuff-links ; here is a skilful bathing-man, to put you through a rousing red-hot bath, and carefully keep your bandaged arm from getting wet ; here are the smiling waiting-maids to serve you with things to eat, strange dishes, pretty to look at, curious to taste, food which seems to satisfy but never banishes the appetite for more than a few moments. Yes, I decide to make the Yao Matsu my hospital and my headquarters and engage a room amid the "Eight Hundred Pine-Trees" for the remainder of my stay.

IN THE RAIN
Photograph by Tamamura

Photograph by Tamamura

"KANJO," THE BILL

My room has balconies on either side ; one is quite narrow and overlooks a sleeping lakelet and the garden ; the other, a broad veranda, serving as a corridor, hangs amid the tree-tops

Photograph by Otis A. Poole

IN A JAPANESE HOTEL

A TRANSPLANTED TOKONOMA

THE VAO MATSU INN

on the river side. **Through** the branches we can see the glimmering waters of the wide Sumidagawa, with here and there a passing junk or sampan sailing cityward. And sometimes when the skies are kind and clear, there rises in the western distance a graceful form like an inverted fan, the far-off, ghost-like apparition of the sacred mountain Fuji-San. My apartment is dainty and immaculate beyond description. Upon the floor are the thick straw-mats called *tatami;* over them rugs are sometimes spread as a precaution against the clumsy destructiveness of "civilized" foreigners. Light, sliding screens covered with translucent paper may at a moment's notice be so disposed as to form several tiny single rooms. One wall of each room is, however, of more substantial stuff. In it is sunk the recess called the "tokonoma," the place to which all ornaments or decorations are confined. In the tokonoma we usually find a bronze or porcelain vase containing flowers, branches of cherry-blossoms or of maple-leaves, or sometimes a dwarfed tree,— a little tree as old as a grandfather, and yet no larger than a child. Against the wall behind is hung the kakemono, or decorated scroll.

The usual impression produced by a Japanese room is one of severe simplicity and cleanliness immaculate. Our first thought on entering one of these airy abodes is that house-cleaning has just been finished, and the furniture not yet been put back in its place.

Photograph by Tamamura

IN FINE WEATHER

The fact that the seemingly bare room contains all necessary furniture is a difficult one to impress upon the Occidental housekeeper. Of course, when meals are served, divers small tables, not more than six inches high, make their appearance, as do also a few lacquer trays. Then at night the beds, or "*futon*," fat, wadded comforters, brought forth from closets dissimulated in the wall, are spread upon the floor ; and if the

Photograph by Tamamura   THE MUKOJIMA AVENUE

night be cold, a little stove called a "*hibachi*" is provided. This is a wooden box, half filled with ashes in which a bit of charcoal is smoldering. If the night be very cold, the traveler may take the stove to bed with him, a perforated cover being put over it to prevent a conflagration.

The neighboring shore of the Sumida River becomes in early spring the favorite resort of the beauty-loving citizens of Tokyo. Then the cherry-trees, which for eleven long, long

By permission

AN IRIS GARDEN

months have stood like ugly skeletons, their denuded bones
outlined against the sky, put forth quite suddenly a wealth of
rosy blossoms, as if to say, "See what I have been secretly

Photograph by Otis A. Poole

CHERRY-BLOSSOMS

preparing. Is not a fortnight of this glory better than months of simple verdure?'' Indeed, the very briefness of the season during which these flowers make the city glad, gives to the cherry-blossoms that charm which only evanescent things possess.

IRIS
Photograph by Otis

Who would not willingly wait a year to see an avenue of trees all glorious with sunset clouds at mid-day ! Japan needs no printed calendar ; her people trace the progress of the seasons in these beauty-festivals that Nature plans and celebrates. The Japanese know, by the token of these flowers, that the spring has come. that March is drawing to a

close, or that the month of April has begun. Travelers who have promised themselves sight of these glories and would insure themselves against a bitter disappointment should reach Japan about the 20th of March, for an early spring and a windy day may bring the cherry-blossom season prematurely to a close ; but as a rule, the middle of the month of April finds the trees still decked. The tree puts all its life and vigor into this one supreme effort in the spring, for it bears no fruit, and through all the other seasons of the year stands bare and leafless, awaiting its next annual glorification. Throughout the land, wherever there are cherry-trees in parks or lanes or temple gardens, the people gather beneath the rosy shade of the lovely but ephemeral flowers, and picnic and poetize until the winds scatter the pretty petals and leave nothing but the remembrance of vanished loveliness. But consolation

WISTARIA

By permission

ENTRANCE TO ASAKUSA PARK

By Permission

ASAKUSA TEMPLE

comes in June, for then the iris flowers spread out their rainbow hues on the green carpets of the gardens which are made even gayer by the dainty dresses of the admiring visitors.

A love of the beautiful is innate in almost every native of Japan. How happy is the nation whose people, even the humblest, can find a satisfying pleasure in the mere contemplation of the things that Nature freely sets before them! And then contrast a dainty tea-house, its wistaria trellises enveloped in purple haze,—with a Teutonic beer-garden, where formal Christmas-trees in hideous green pots are ranged in rows!

The Japa-nese are in close and loving con-verse at all sea-sons with Dame Nature and she responds to their affection. When wooed by a gardener of this race, she yields delightful and astonishing proofs of her love for the peo-ple of the Land of Flowers. The Japanese regard the art of our florists as

THE ASAKUSA TOWER

barbarous, thinking a flower too
precious a thing to be crowded
with a score of others into a
basket or bouquet, or
massed to form atrocious
"floral designs"—an-
chors, broken columns,
or "gates ajar!" One
flower in one vase is
very Japanese, and
after we have studied
the charming effects at-
tained through simplicity,
we come to look upon our
own methods of floral arrange-
ment as distasteful and wasteful.

A MATSURI CAR

Then in November come the chrysanthemums — the
National Flower of Japan. The chrysanthemums do not
grow along the roadside, but must be sought in the gardens

MATSURI SEASON

Photograph by Otis A. Poole

FOR THE WEE ONES

of the expert florists where, in dainty greenhouses of bamboo and under roofs of delicate oiled paper, they spread their gorgeous petals to delight the eyes of multitudes who flock to these exhibitions of the gardener's art. The finest are to be seen in the Imperial Gardens at Tokyo, and fortunately an invitation to the Mikado's Garden-Party gave me an opportunity to see this celebrated display. On one single stem I saw no fewer than four hundred and sixty-five perfect blossoms, and where other stems bore but a single flower, each was a marvel in size and coloring.

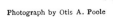

Photograph by Otis A. Poole

" LOVE ME, LOVE MY DOG "

One of my earliest outings is a visit to Asakusa. There is always a crowd at Asakusa ; it is the most popular resort of Tokyo. People come to pray and play. Religion and merriment hold joint sway over this celebrated quarter. There are a dozen shrines and temples, there are a hundred dozen shops and shows. But first, like pious Buddhists, let us go to the great Temple of the Mercy Goddess, Kwannon, clap our hands before her image, add one metallic drop to the never-ceasing rain of copper coin that pours from the clouds of superstition into her treasure troughs, and with our remaining fractions of a cent buy grain and seed from the old woman in the court to feed the hungry pigeons which dwell beneath the eaves of the temple. Then, after climbing the ugly

Photograph by Otis A. Poole

THE LANTERN-MAKER

twelve-story tower, we return to the city streets, to find a festival, or *"matsuri,"* in progress. These matsuri seem to break out on the slightest provocation. An entire quarter will suddenly, for no obvious reason, "shut up shop" and

By Permission

STREET-CARS NEAR UYENO

give itself over to rejoicings and enjoyment. A gigantic car of several stories is drawn through the streets attended by the happy crowds. Upon the higher platforms are mummers and musicians ; and on top of all an effigy of some old warrior or hero. Just what the fuss is all about the stranger never knows. We are content to take the celebration as a picturesque event, and to let its mythical, religious, or historical meaning remain a mystery. Child life is never seen to such advantage as during these days of popular jubilation. The quaintest, cutest little types of Japaninity parade the streets in festival attire. A whole lecture might be given on the "Wee Ones of Japan," and should it ever be my privilege to come again to this land of happy childhood, I promise you that I shall not fail to study this delightful subject. The stranger always has ample warning that a matsuri is coming. Two or three days before the arrival of the happy date the streets of all the quarter blossom out with paper lanterns,

IN UYENO PARK

uniform in shape and in design according to the special fête-day to be celebrated. At night the scene is one of fairy-land. Interminable double rows of glowing lanterns stretch away in all directions. In any other land these lanterns would be made by machinery in gigantic factories; in Japan they are made by hand in tiny studios, for lantern-making is not an industry, it is an art. This is the secret of the charm of "things Japanese." The factories are studios, the in-dustries are arts, and the workmen, almost without excep-tion, artists. Many of my photographic slides were colored by a little man whose daily pay would not equal that of the "artist" who whitewashes our fences. The ability of skilled, artistic, Japanese labor to under-live even the common toilers

of the West is the most threatening feature of Japanese competition in the markets of the world.   It is, however, devoutly
to be wished that industrial and commercial progress shall not
mean artistic degeneration, and the annihilation of Japan's
innate good taste.   It gives us a shock every time we meet a
street-car here in Tokyo ; they are abominably out of place,
exasperatingly deliberate, usually overcrowded, and astonish-
ingly cheap.   It is almost a day's journey to cross the big
metropolis in one of those slow cars.   The picturesque,
speedy, and exclusive rikisha is comparatively expensive, but
let us hope that it will successfully resist its rival, for a Japanese city without it would be indeed a sorry place.

But the beauties of Uyeno Park, especially in springtime,
make amends for the ugly banality of modern means of reach-
ing it.   Once within the limits of the park, we find ourselves
again in old Japan.   Uyeno, like Asakusa, is a place of prayer
and picnics.   Crowds throng into the temple courts, and the

GARDEN OF THE CHA-YA

tramp of many feet shod with wooden sandals when falling on the granite paths makes a strange music, a sound peculiar to Japan. It may be likened to the sound that would be made by a large orchestra composed entirely of xylophones. The Japanese are a nation of picnickers; but what people would not go

THE MAGYASU
ĖA-HOUSE, TOKYO

in for frequent picnics, given these same inducements—a perpetual round of floral festivals? The blossoming of the cherry-tree, the advent of the iris, the drooping of the wistaria,—all these events call out this beauty-loving population to gardens, parks, or favorite tea-houses, famous for some special flower.

But there is one perennial attraction to every tea-house in Japan, that of the pretty "Geisha," about whom so much has been said, and about whom so little is accurately known In that dainty musical comedy, called "The Geisha," so well presented by the late Augustin Daly's Company, we had a picture of tea-house life as it appears

Photograph by Nagasaki

CHUMS

to many travelers. The heroine, a pretty dancing-girl, flirts with the foreign visitors, attracting custom to the chaya, of which she is the bright, particular star ; but her smiles and winks dispensed to patrons mean no more than do the smiles and winks that come to us across the footlights. It is all acting, made more difficult because there are no footlights to help out the artist, and no curtain to ring down when her

SHIMBASHI GEISHA

trying scene is done. The art of being a geisha is the art of being perpetually and convincingly amiable. Who will deny that this is the most difficult of all the arts ? Yet trained to it from childhood the geisha of Japan succeed so well that their life seems one of unaffected happy, girlish gaiety. But behind it all there are long hours of hard work at the "samisen," with singing teachers, with the costumer and dancing-master.

The geisha are not attached to the staff of the tea-house, but are sent for when ordered by the guests for whom they are to dance and sing. The younger geisha are doll-like children, for most of those who dance are children from twelve to fifteen years of age ; those who play the musical accompaniments are older, but not over nineteen at the most. The remuneration they receive is indeed very small.

MONKEYS

It may be that these little creatures are not beautiful according to our western standards, but no one can deny that they possess a strange, exotic charm ; they seem unreal, impossible, mysterious. They are one moment like playful, romping children, thoughtless and wild, the next like women, strangely youthful, strangely dignified, as if conscious of their charm. Or, again, at some stately banquet, they may appear impassive as priestesses, pouring saké from graceful porcelain bottles as if they were performing some religious rite. It has been said that there is no expression in the faces of the Japanese. "They are

GREETING

like monkeys," says one critic. I beg to differ with him. Here are monkeys, the most famous in Japan, carved on a sacred structure by a classic sculptor of three hundred years ago. The group is meant to teach the pious lesson that we should neither speak, hear, nor see any evil. Let us ask a clever little geisha to imitate as closely as she can the expressions and the poses of these tricentenarian simians. First the middle one, who is supposed to *speak* no evil. Not difficult this; for there are no evil words in Japanese, no words profane, no words that soil the lips. She must learn the speech of Shakespeare or of Molière, before she can speak evil. And now she stops the ears that she may *hear* no evil; needless precaution. Lafcadio Hearn says that he lived more than a year in Japan without hearing an angry word pronounced, or witnessing a real quarrel. And finally, that she may *see* no evil, let her hide her almond eyes behind her chubby fingers.

True there is evil to be seen in every land, and in Japan the evil most conspicuous is that which we champions of Western civilization have ourselves introduced. But to return to our monkeys—if these be monkeys, we might all beg to be put in the cage!

Geisha are, in fact, the most important part of a Japanese feast. Without geisha no entertainment in good society could possibly be given with success. They are not waitresses, however; they are artists, proficient in the art of entertaining and always clever, pretty, and well-gowned. True they do serve both food and saké; but this they do artistically, not as servants, but with the grace and graciousness of hostesses. A gentleman giving a dinner to his

THE TOKYO OF TO-DAY

friends would never dream of permitting his wife to do the honors. She probably would not be seen. A group of geisha would be engaged to furnish that pervading feminine charm without which a feast is nothing. The geisha are expected to enliven conversation, amuse the guests with witty sayings and bright stories, delight them with pretty mannerisms, all this time keeping the saké cups well filled. Saké, which is distilled from rice, is usually served warm in

By permission

GEISHA

GEISHA TEACHING FOREIGNERS TO DANCE

tiny porcelain bowls, holding about four thimblefuls. Though it is but mildly alcoholic, its effects must be most agreeable, according to a native drinking song which may be translated somewhat as follows:

> " When you drink saké,
> You feel like the springtime.
> And the loud cries
> Of impatient creditors
> On the outside,
> Sound in your ears
> Like the voices of nightingales
> Singing most sweetly."

Photograph by Otis A. Poole

A SHOP-FRONT

Between the courses of the dinner or at the conclusion the geisha perform descriptive dances, strangely graceful, and ranging from slow and solemn, almost religious movements, to indescribable flutterings, like those of colored butterflies.

These pantomimic dances each tell some pretty story, poetic or historic. The plot, however, is difficult to grasp, nor is our comprehension facilitated by the explanations of our guide, who actually thought that he had elucidated everything with the following words: "Gentlemen, I will explain him" ("him," meaning, of course, the plot). "Long time ago Daimio he come to beach with his ladies.

A BAMBOO WALL
Photograph by Otis A. Poole

He think he saw a poem, so she went to his home and destroy his enemy with the poem and the general—he was a very bad man." And then we said, "Ah, yes; how interesting!" Of course the geisha play the inevitable, distressing samisen, and sing their little songs. This is distinctly less agreeable, for such squeaks and squeals as issue from their pretty lips in the name of heaven-sent harmony are enough to break the spell that their soft gentle tones, employed in conversation, have cast about our spirits. Some one has written apropos of this, "It is quite fortunate that the musical art is not more generally practiced in Japan." And to this the average, uncomprehending Westerner must add, "Amen!" For although these Oriental maidens may fascinate the Western eye, they can do nothing but exasperate the Western ear when they burst into song. Like good little children, they should be seen and not heard.

Let us, then, go out into the streets where we may see them by the score. How may we best describe these busy streets? They are so strange, so changing, so bizarre. It seems as if the population had nothing to do but wander up and down to add life and color to these Oriental thoroughfares. True, the effect of this Eastern picture is now and then marred by the passing of a mousmé, bearing a hideous modern parasol imported from the West, or by the fleeting presence of some Oriental gentleman whose artistic costume is crowned by a derby hat of antiquated form. These are, however, insignificant defects. The picture in the ensemble is delightful, and we never tire of the pretty sights that greet us as we dash in rikishas through these crowded streets, our

ENTRANCE TO THE MIKADO'S PALACE

runners pushing loiterers aside, because they think that foreign passengers are always in a hurry. There are few streets, even in the larger cities, that bear the impress of foreign architectural teaching, although here and there we find an ugly building in the modern style ; and in these streets there is comparatively little stir and noise, no genuinely heavy traffic, no rumbling trucks, no feverish haste. Instead of these we find the swift and almost noiseless flight of rikishas, at times a gentle flutter of excitement, perhaps a little polite crowding, and over all a sound like that of laughter, broken

now and then by cheerful cries.   Even a funeral should not
be a sad spectacle.   The exquisite courtesy of the Japanese
teaches them that it is rude and selfish to show a sad face to
the world.   They are taught to bear grief with a smiling face.
We are told of the foreigner who was shocked by what
seemed to him the heartlessness of the family nurse, who
announced to him the death of her husband with a low laugh
and a smiling face.   In reality that laugh betokened the most
thoughtful consideration for the master.   To have appeared
before the master with an unpleasant tear-stained face, to
have addressed him with the tones of woe, would have been
impolite.   The laugh that accompanies the announcement
of sad news has been translated into words by Mr. Hearn.
It signifies, "This you might honorably think to be an
unhappy event.   Pray do not suffer Your Superiority to feel
concerned about so inferior a matter, and pardon the neces-
sity which causes us to outrage politeness by speaking about
such an affair at all."   The Japanese speak of the angry

EXQUISITE CARPENTRY

Photograph by Otis A. Poole

E OF THE MOATS
otograph by Otis A. Poole

faces of the foreigner, and ask why it is that we so seldom smile. Children in the remoter provinces always cry out in terror when they see for the first time the features of a European. In the early days the strong-featured faces of the foreigners were likened to the faces of demons. It must be confessed that Occidental physiognomy lacks the reposeful calmness so characteristic of the Orient.

The home of Japanese Majesty is an unseen palace hidden in the depths of a vast, silent, almost impenetrable park ; for around it rise three series of cyclopean walls crowned with castle-like turrets and protected by broad deep moats. Though situated in the very center of Japan's greatest city, this imperial abode is as silent as the grave ; for so thick are the ramparts and so broad the moats that none of the turmoil of the outer world may penetrate to the inner gardens where the Emperor, surrounded by his court, dwells in a semi-religious seclusion. Although formerly invisible to his people, the

Photograph by Otis A. Poole

LEARNING WESTERN WAYS

Emperor now frequently shows himself in public. At the annual garden-party, held in the grounds of another and less sacred palace, in November, 1892, I had the honor of meeting face to face the Mikado, Mutsu Hito, the Empress, and some thirty of the ladies of the court. Of course no pictures of the scene were in any way obtainable. Fortunately so, perhaps, for alas! all who come to the state-functions must obey the imperial mandate and appear in modern European dress. Would that the Japanese of high degree could see themselves as others see them at the garden-party. The imperial court has lost much in dignity by abandoning the artistic dress of old Japan in favor of the hideous habiliments of Western civilization. The little Empress of Japan, O Haru, a woman of the most refined, aristocratic type, looked sadly ill at ease in her gown fresh from Paris. She and the dainty ladies of the court seemed to have laid aside their grace and poise together with their fine old robes of state. The Empress shook the hands of those who were presented to her, like a timid school-girl; and the bows of the court ladies, so graceful when performed in native costume, are rendered comic when every forward inclination of the body is attended by the skyward bobbing of an antiquated bustle. Nor can the men, any more than the women of Japan, wear gracefully the costumes of the West. Even

GOWNED IN THE FASHION

the Emperor, arrayed in a military uniform like those affected
by European monarchs, seemed to lack, because of certain
inherited mannorisms, that peculiar quality which we are
pleased to call "a kingly bearing." His innate dignity,

Photograph by Enami

IN SHIBA'S SHADE

however, would have impressed us had he appeared in the
superb Japanese robes of state like those worn by his imperial
ancestors and even by himself before the Restoration. The
coats of many of the guests revealed curious conceptions
of foreign fashions. Nor was their headgear less remarkable.
The relative sizes of hat and head had apparently never been
taken into consideration. In many cases the hats were of
such generous proportions that they were prevented from
settling to the wearer's shoulders, and thus eclipsing his
countenance, only by resting on his diplomatic ears. Fortunately this craze for foreign dress, that at one time threatened

to pervade all classes, is now confined to the small circle of the "upper ten." At court the wearing of it is obligatory, but the people have realized that the adoption of European dress without the adoption of European manners is incongruous and silly. The good sense of the mousmé of Japan prompts her to retain her graceful native dress that gives her that indefinable charm to which not only famous poets but also mere travelers have alike been subject. "But the Japanese girl turns in her toes," some may say. What if she does? She does it gracefully, and they are very pretty toes, because they have not been deformed by leather shoes. "Trilby" could never have become famous in Japan merely because her feet were natural in shape. The Japanese girl, when she bows, bends forward from the waist, at the same time gliding her hands downward to her knees, then straightens up again. This movement, awkward when performed by foreigners, is, when done by those who know its secret, as graceful as the prettiest of Occidental curtsies. Her taste

REGIMENTS OF TORO

Photograph by Kimbei

STONE LANTERNS

in matters of raiment is usually exquisite and almost invariably good.   Bad taste is hardly ever manifested by the Japanese save when they affect the things that are not Japanese.

But to resume our rambles in the capital.   We make our way to the sacred park of Shiba, the burial-place of the last of the Shoguns, the last of those great generals of the Tokugawa family who previous to 1868 dwelt in the palace of Tokyo and there held temporal sway, while the reigning Mikado lived the life of a demigod in inglorious tranquillity, in far away Kyoto.   The one feature of this sacred park most vividly recalled is the great army of tall, mysterious stone lanterns — "*toro*," as they are called.   Thousands and thousands of them stand in close ranks about the graveled courts.   To us they seem like a host of ancient warriors waiting to attend some solemn ceremony in honor of their departed Prince ; and this simile is not inapt.   For each of these lanterns was erected here by some great daimio, or noble, owing feudal service to the Tokugawas. And thus these immobile battalions truly represent the military strength of the old warrior whose funeral court they guard. The tombs of these Tokugawa Princes are surrounded by shrines and temples that are among the most magnificent in all Japan. The Japanese delight in honoring their military chiefs as gods, and all this deification and worship of old heroes is only the survival of that admirable spirit of loyalty to lords and princes that was the key-note of the feudal life. This land has had a noble and chivalrous past, as is proved by many tales of bravery and daring, and of these tales of chivalry none is more popular than the famous story of "The Forty-seven Ronin." Almost two hundred years ago a certain Kotsuké, a cowardly favorite of the Shogun, after insulting the noble Prince Ako, not only refused him satisfaction, but, to avoid a duel, obtained by perfidy from the Shogun a condemnation of Prince Ako and the seizure of his lands and castles. Ako, obedient to the Shogun's s e n t e n c e, committed suicide by h a r a kiri.

GATE AND PAGODA OF SHIBA

At this, the retainers of the martyred prince declared themselves "Ronin" or "masterless men," and swore to avenge Prince Ako's death. But the crafty Kotsuké guarded well his person. The Ronin were compelled to bide their time. To allay suspicion they feigned indifference, and, abandoning wives and children, pretended to lead dissolute and careless lives. But all this time they were perfecting plans of vengeance, and for many years in profoundest secrecy

Photograph by Enami

GRAVES OF THE RONIN

they awaited the day of reckoning. At last the day of reckoning arrived. Kotsuké becoming careless from long security, reduced his guard, and one winter night the band of Ronin broke into his palace, slew his retainers and, capturing their cowardly enemy alive, demanded that he should end his life by suicide, as their master had been forced to do. But he had not the courage to do the bidding of the avengers, who therefore severed his head from his body, and laid it some hours later as an offering on Prince Ako's tomb.

To-day that grave is surrounded by forty-seven other graves. For, the vendetta accomplished, the Ronin gave themselves up to justice. Their deed was lauded to the skies ; but feudal law required that they should die. To them, however, was granted the privilege of that death, dear to the chivalric Samurai, the "happy dispatch," or hara kiri. Thus the forty-seven Ronin with their own daggers stoically disemboweled themselves, and falling forward in their own lifeblood, died with their master's name upon their lips.

And now after two centuries have passed, this burial court is still a place of pilgrimage. Here, as in a temple, rise clouds of incense offered up before the tombs by a never-ending procession of visitors, who come from far and near to pay their tribute to the loyalty and courage of these forty-seven men who died because their master's name and honor were to them the most sacred things on earth.

This story in its dramatic form is one of the most popular of the native dramas, and is repeated often at the Japanese play-houses. It is as familiar to the Japanese theater-goers as "Hamlet" is to us. It was my privilege to see it admirably presented by the famous Danjiro, the greatest actor of Japan, an artist who ranks among the great dramatic geniuses of modern times. Although the stage-traditions and customs of the Japanese differ widely from our own, a Japanese drama may be comprehended and enjoyed even by one who

GRAVESTONES

Photograph by Ogawa

HARA KIRI

does not know the language of the players. Many scenes are done almost entirely in pantomime with an accompaniment of music and recitative. The stage-settings and the costumes are magnificent; and realism is carried far beyond anything with which we are familiar. Take, for example, the suicide of good Prince Ako; we are not spared a single phase of his death-agony. Like the brave Samurai he is, Prince Ako, condemned by his sovereign, dies preferably by his own hand.

In old Japan hara kiri was the only honorable death for a man in disgrace. The victim, dressed always in white, attended by his second, and in the presence of the appointed witnesses, grasps a small dirk, and at a signal thrusts it into his body. Then with the knife in his vitals he must deliver his last messages to his friend and second, and then complete his work with a quick side-movement of the blade, thus disemboweling himself. Should he lack strength or courage for this final effort, it is the duty of his second to decapitate him instantaneously with a long curved sword. To learn to perform gracefully both of these strokes was formerly a part of every noble's education, and boys were early exercised in the approved method of holding and thrusting the self-destroying dirk and of swinging the executionary sword.

A THEATER

The scenes of the play are changed with great rapidity. When an act is finished, the curtain is not drawn, but the stage-setting and the actors in their final poses are mechanically whirled out of sight. The entire stage revolves like a gigantic turn-table, and the new scene that has been prepared on the rear half of the platform is swung around and presented to the audience. The actors who are to take part in it are already in position to begin their business. Those who make their entrances later in the scene do not appear from the wings, but come stalking in from the back of the parquet circle down a narrow elevated aisle ; sometimes making long speeches before they reach the stage.

There are, of course, no chairs or seats of any kind in the auditorium. The parquet is merely a sloping floor divided into little trays or boxes of about four square feet by railings about eight inches high. For comfort's sake I came to the matinée in native costume. My faithful servitor, Tsuni Horiuchi, had secured one of those little trays, and in it we wedged ourselves. Throughout two acts I sat successfully in Japanese fashion, my legs shut up beneath me. During the

By permission   A STREET OF SHOWS

third act, however, my Occidental muscles unused to this Oriental stretching begin to warn me that the end is near. I whisper to my boy that I must straighten out my legs or die ; but *how?* — that is the question. There is no room. "I will buy room for your honorable feet," he answers ; and rushing out he returns with tickets for the vacant box in front of us. Then gently unfolding my stiffened members, he draws my feet carefully under the intervening rail and deposes them, toes pointing skyward, in the middle of that adjoining box.

Photograph by Enami

A WRESTLING TOURNAMENT

We boldly meet the amused smiles of the spectators, and like them, proceed to order tea and saké, and also soups and omelettes, — for the play lasts from early morning until dark, and everybody is expected to have one or more meals brought in from the tea-houses which serve also as ticket agencies.

Leaving the theater, we go in search of more exciting entertainment at the wrestling-pavilion. A pair of brawny braves are about to test their powers before an admiring public. What boxing is to the Anglo-Saxon, and fencing to the Frenchman, such is wrestling to the Japanese. The wrestlers are a class apart, recruited from among the big men of the land where little people are the rule. Fat, rather than muscular in appearance, they depend more on sheer brute-force and weight than on agility and skill, the object being to tumble one's opponent out of the ring as expeditiously as possible. But our interest in this rude sport soon flags, and we depart to prepare for our journey from Tokyo to the western Capital, Kyoto, three hundred miles away. We shall, however, travel leisurely and with many lingerings.

The country through which we are now to make our way is one of the greenest countries in the world. In every traveler's note-book the word "green" is repeated time and again on every page. At certain seasons of the year Japan, from end to end, is one long, beautiful, entrancing symphony in green. It is the Emerald Isle of the Orient, — an Emerald Isle without potatoes, famine, shillalahs, or oppression, for in Japan potatoes are an unknown quantity, famine is happily a stranger, and the people, while eminently courageous, are not pugnacious, nor have they ever had cause to resist oppression. Let me quote a few words from one of the books of Lafcadio Hearn, than whom no foreigner knows more about Japan or more truly understands the nature of the Japanese. It is not too much to say that those who have never read his books do not and cannot know the real Japan. He writes: "I have been fourteen months in a certain

A WRESTLER

province, and I have not yet heard voices raised in anger or
witnessed a quarrel ; never have I seen one man strike another,
or a woman bullied, or a child slapped.   Indeed, I have never
seen any real roughness anywhere that I have been in Japan,
except at the open ports where the poorer classes seem, through
contact with Europeans, to lose their natural politeness,—their
native morals,—even their capacity for simple happiness.''

Photograph by Otis A. Poole

'' WHERE ALL MOVEMENT IS SLOW AND SOFT ''

And this is literally true.   Again he speaks of ''The supremely
pleasurable impression produced by the singular gentleness of
popular scrutiny.''   He says : '' Everybody looks at you curiously, but there is never anything disagreeable, much less hos-
tile, in the gaze.   Most commonly it is accompanied by a smile
or half smile, and the ultimate consequence of all these kindly
curious looks is that the stranger finds himself thinking of fairy-
land.   Hackneyed to the degree of provocation this statement

no doubt is. Everybody describing his first Japanese day talks of the land as 'Fairy-land' and of its people as 'Fairy-folk'; yet there is a natural reason for this unanimity in the choice of terms to describe what is almost impossible to describe more accurately. To find one's self suddenly in a world where everything is upon a smaller and daintier scale than with us,—a world of lesser and seemingly kindlier beings, all smiling at you as if to wish you well; a world where all

Photograph by Otis A. Poole

NOON

movement is slow and soft and voices are hushed; a world where land, life, and sky are unlike what one has known elsewhere—this is surely the realization, for imaginations nourished with English folk-lore, of the old dream of a world of elves."

Again, he asks, and with good cause, "Where are the outward, material signs of that immense new force that Japan has been showing both in productivity and in war? Nowhere. The land remains what it was before. Its face has scarcely been modified by all the changes of the present period. The miniature railways and telegraph-poles, the bridges and tunnels, might almost escape notice in the ancient green of the landscapes. You might journey two hundred miles through the interior, looking in vain for large manifestations of the new civilization. A Japanese city is still what it was centuries ago—little more than a wilderness of wooden sheds, picturesque, indeed, as paper lanterns are, but scarcely less frail.''

A visit to the site of Kamakura will show us that this is true, for Kamakura, once the greatest city of Japan, has almost vanished from the land. During the comparatively

THE KAMAKURA BUDDHA FROM THE RICE-FIELDS

brief period of her written history, Japan has had more than sixty capitals, of which the greater number have completely disappeared. Kamakura is only one of those threescore of imperial cities that have passed into oblivion. But to the former greatness of the place one thing bears enduring testimony,—it is the Dai Butsu, a gigantic bronze image of Gautama Buddha, the most impressive, awe-inspiring monument in all Japan, nay, more—in all the Orient. We are told that it is fifty feet in height, the face from ear to ear is seventeen, an eye, four feet across, and that within the image is a chamber where more than a hundred men may kneel in prayer. But all these details add nothing to our admiration for this great medieval work. Its very presence inspires awe and reverence. It stands the symbol of a great religion, and is to educated Buddhists in no sense an idol. Sadly at variance with the grand teachings of Buddhism are many of the practices and superstitions which now dim the "Light of Asia." But just as the lotus-flower rises from the slime in purity and

Photograph by Otis A. Poole

LOTUS

beauty, so do the great, pure thoughts of Buddha stand forth from the mists of superstition in which the cult has long been shrouded. Why the lotus has become the symbolic flower of the Buddhist faith has been told us in graceful words in the English composition of a Japanese school-boy who writes :

"Though growing in the foulest slime, the flower remains pure and undefiled.

"And the soul of him who remains ever pure in the midst of temptation is likened unto the lotus.

"Therefore is the lotus carved or painted upon the furniture of temples ; therefore also does it appear in all the representations of our Lord Buddha.

"In paradise the blessed shall sit at ease enthroned upon the cups of golden lotus-flowers."

The Dai Butsu has sat here in silent contemplation for more than seven centuries. Once it stood in the heart of a great city; now it looks out upon the abandoned site of Kamakura, the vanished capital. Almost a million people once dwelt round about it ; what were the busy streets of long ago are now become grassy lanes. A mere village bears the proud title of Kamakura,—thatched huts and rice-fields have succeeded the imperial palaces and gardens,—the Japanese

Photograph by Kimbei

PROFILE OF THE DAI BUTSU

metropolis of seven hundred years ago, the home of the old Emperors, has disappeared. All, save the temples and this mighty figure, has been destroyed by time and war and flood and fire. Four centuries ago the Buddha sat within a gorgeous temple. In 1494 a tidal-wave rushed inland from the neighboring bay, swept away the sheltering temple; and with the débris of an engulfed city bore it out to sea. But neither this catastrophe nor the innumerable wars and confla-

THE FACE OF
THE GREAT BUDDHA

grations that have raged round this imperishable form have disturbed the eternal serenity of the face so divinely calm, nor caused a quiver of the half-closed lids beneath which sleep great eyes of gold. In these bronze features there is a something supernatural that by its mystery both fascinates and awes us.

As I stood for the first time in this great presence, I thought to comprehend, though dimly, the calm that comes of

Photograph by Otis A. Poole

BUDDHA'S NEIGHBORS

Photograph by O. M. Poole

SAILS ON THE SEA

self-annihilation and perfected knowledge, the calm that is
reflected in the face of the Dai Butsu.   The slow succession of
the centuries and the swift march of events have left no trace

AT ENOSHIMA

upon this changeless countenance. Nay, more,—those eyes
of the Great Buddha, though on a level with the treetops,
were not even raised to look out seaward upon that strange
fleet, called "the black ships," which half a century ago
approached this land under the guidance of our famous Perry.

Yet well might the Buddha have taken heed of them,
for they were bringing to Japan undreamed-of changes, and a
future full of progress and of turmoil. Their coming was the

THE WAY TO ENOSHIMA

signal that Japan's period of peace and isolation was drawing to a close. Our ships brought to the Japanese a thousand new responsibilities, which were accepted at first with
reluctance, then with willingness ; and now for the first time
in the history of nations a dark-skinned people has assumed
and is bearing worthily the "white man's burden."

Continuing our journey we visit briefly the lovely island of
Enoshima with its high-perched yadoyas and temples and
then travel slowly westward along the old Tokaido, or

FROM AN INN AT ENOSHIMA

ON THE TOKAIDO

PILGRIMS

"Highway of the Eastern Sea." This was once the most frequented route between the eastern and the western capitals, and throughout its entire course of three hundred miles it was paralleled by a continuous series of villages of shops and inns and lodging-places for the retinues of traveling princes. To-day the daimio, or nobles, are whirled from Tokyo to Kyoto in modern railway-cars, and the Tokaido, once so brilliant and so full of life, is

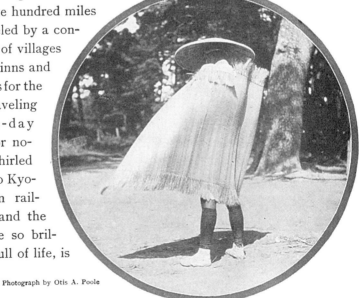

A PILGRIM'S WATERPROOF

deserted save by the poorest peasants and the most eccentric
travelers.   The highway leads us soon into the Hakoné
Mountains, to Miyanoshita, the favorite summering-place of
foreigners and natives.   But we are not concerned with the

PROSPEROUS PEASANTRY

luxurious semi-European hotels ; delightful as they are, they
are not Japanese.   Instead of idling on their broad verandas,
we go forth on foot to see what we may see.   And everywhere we see the homes of industry and honest toil, surrounded by fields minutely cultivated.   The farmers' houses
have heavy roofs of thatch with little strips of growing
verdure on the ridges.   Beneath the eaves hang golden
fringes made of yellowing ears of corn.

The interiors are as clean, as chastely simple, as in the
houses of the rich.   Housekeeping must be indeed a pleasure
to the women in Japan, for there is no bric-à-brac to break,

no untidy "tidies" to get mussed, no furniture to move, nothing but mats of
straw to sweep and sliding screens
on which to paste occasionally a
sheet of fresh white paper.   So
little housework is there to be
done that the farmers' wives
devote themselves to agricultural toil, and we look with
admiration on the sturdy
peasant women who labor
all day in the open fields.
Some of them are threshing
rice, one handful at a time, by
drawing it across a sort of metal
comb.   And thinking of our patent threshers, we marvel at this

THRESHING

INDUSTRY

Photographs by Otis A. Poole

people so rich in patience, so poor in all things else.   Yet I
doubt if there be a land where content dwells more intimately
among the poorer classes than here in the "Land of Rice-
Ears."   And the courtesy of even the humblest of the

ROADSIDE COURTESIES

peasants gives us a feeling of absolute security amid these
gentle, happy-humored people.   In these valleys, tea-houses,
or roadside resting-places, are as numerous as elsewhere in
Japan.   Never are we suffered to approach without a welcome.   The hostess always bustles out and greets us with
low bows, and as she bows, she makes a curious hissing
sound by drawing in her breath through her closed teeth.
At first it is a little disconcerting to be greeted everywhere by
this sound like that of escaping steam, but it is always so ;
whenever we approach an inn some one apparently turns on
the human radiators which continue to sizzle until long after

we have been comfortably installed. And these oft-repeated sniffs are not a sign of influenza ; they are an outward and audible sign of an inward and healthy politeness. They mean that we are very welcome. I always tried to return these greetings with interest and soon became proficient in the back-breaking bow of Dai Nippon and could hold my own with any of them in a hissing contest. But not everywhere are we greeted with smiles, as is proved by the picture

Photograph by **Enami**

HAKONE

of the glaring stone god that greeted us as we approached another village. That unhappy deity sits at the roadside, his significance a mystery. But after a careful study of his expression and attitude of anguish, and the suggestive position of his hands, tightly clasped over his stomach, we decide that he can be none other than the "God of

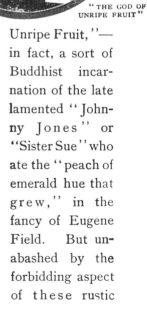

"THE GOD OF UNRIPE FRUIT"

Unripe Fruit,"— in fact, a sort of Buddhist incarnation of the late lamented "Johnny Jones" or "Sister Sue" who ate the "peach of emerald hue that grew," in the fancy of Eugene Field. But unabashed by the forbidding aspect of these rustic

A TEMPLE STAIRWAY

VOTIVE SANDALS

gods, I continued to look after my spiritual welfare by attending church on every possible occasion. Nor is salvation lightly to be obtained in Japan.

A picture of the front steps of one of the temples will convince you that frequent church-going in this region is more or less fatiguing; still, we religiously mount every tier of steps to do homage, not to the local deity, but to the Goddess of the Picturesque who sits enshrined alike in Shinto and in Buddhist temples. And our ardor in her service is well recompensed, for never do we climb in vain, invariably finding something worth the labor. Much that is grotesque to foreigners is mingled with that which is naïve and charming. For instance, we discover a votive-offering that is nothing less than a pair of Japanese shoes or waraji, three feet long, made of heavy metal. We are told that these enormous shoes were the

A NEW USE FOR NATIVE SANDALS

offering of an ambitious jinrikisha runner who desired to excel
in speed and endurance all other kurumayas as signally as
these shoes excel in size and weight all the waraji of Japan.

A SPECIAL KAGO

Stout legs are an advantage even for foreign visitors to this
mountain region, where those who cannot walk become the
victims of the "ka-
go" and its kindred
instruments of tor-
ture.

The kago is not
a complicated sort of
conveyance, but it is
one that requires long
training on the part
of its would-be occu-
pant. Absolutely no
provision has been
made for Occidental
legs, which are both
much longer and less

CARRYING HIS CAB

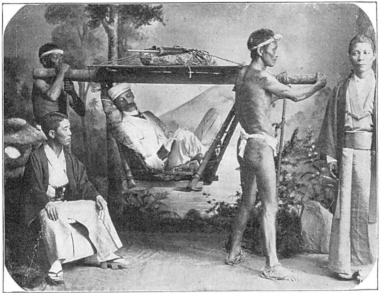

Photograph by Tamamura   MY FRIEND FROM MINNEAPOLIS

THE OTOMÉ TOGE

Photograph by O. M. Poole

FUJI

flexible than the Oriental article. A Japanese when riding
in a kago sits on his legs, but the foreigner, unless willing

Photograph by O. M. Poole

FUJI

to submit to amputation, is advised to walk or else remain at home. The men who carry kagos carry little else, save a long staff and a skin so beautifully tattooed that the passenger may while away the weary miles in studying the intricate designs upon the bearer's back. A suit of tattoo is ample clothing for a summer day. In fact, it is an ideal hot-weather

Photograph by O. M. Poole

FUJI

costume. It cannot be denied that it fits well, lasts a life-time, and that it will never fade and never shrink.

As a closing experience in the Hakoné region, we climb to the famous mountain-pass called the "Otomé Togé." This is one of the gateways leading from the Hakoné valleys to the broader valley from which the sacred mountain Fuji-no-Yama rises in one grand sweep. The Japanese speak of their

sacred mountain not as Fuji-Yama, but either as Fuji-no-
Yama, "Mountain of Fuji," or more commonly and lovingly
as Fuji San. The beautiful mountain is twelve thousand
three hundred and sixty-five feet high. To view the
sacred summit from the Otomé pass is the ambition of every
traveler, but seldom is it possible to realize it perfectly, for as
a rule she hides her snow-cone in a hood of clouds or vapor,

Photograph by Tamamura

FUJI-NO-YAMA

exposing to disappointed eyes only the lower slopes which
look like a vast inclined plane leading from earth to heaven.

To-day, however, fortune favors us, and Fuji San stands
there, revealed in her most somber wintry aspect. Here
for a moment let us indulge in that esthetic pastime of
the cultured Japanese, called "Fuji-viewing." Ethereal
indeed this lovely mountain! Even on near approach it

seems intangible, as if it were but an illusion built of violet
mist and flecked with slender drifts of cloud. In summer
Fuji wears a dainty crown of silver, and a diaphanous robe of
shadowy blue. In winter Fuji shrouds herself in a white
mantle that sometimes trails its icy hem in the green valleys
round about. But Fuji is not always robed in blue and white;
moments there are when the sacred mountain is transfigured
by the glory of the sky. At sunset she stands forth in gorgeous purple against a golden background—at sunrise a pink
halo hovers turban-like round her head, and as the dawn
advances, a pinkish veil unfolds and falls upon her snowy
shoulders. Then gradually the morning colors fade, the violet
mist rises from the valleys and, on the summit, fearfully far
above us, the snow gleams white and pure in the light of a
noonday sun. But even brighter is the gleaming of the snow
crown of the mountain mirrored in the surrounding lakes.

A FOOT-BRIDGE

OUR EXPEDITION

A submarine Fuji is evoked by every lake or placid stream, and oftentimes the unreal inverted vision is more beautiful than the reality, unreal as that reality may seem.

The great charm of Japan lies in the seeming unreality of things. I did not climb this mountain lest the charm be lost.

Photograph by Otis A. Poole

TEA-HOUSE DRAPED WITH BANNERS LEFT BY FUJI PILGRIMS

I did not care to learn that it is nothing but a gritty ash-heap piled more than twelve thousand feet above the sea. Those great magicians, light, atmosphere, and distance, transmute the mass of ash and lava into a radiant vision of loveliness and grandeur. Let us remember it as such. Surely no earthly memory can give us purer pleasure. But even were we disposed to climb, the season is too far advanced for us to dream

WAITING FOR THE TRAIN

of an ascent. In July and August the mountain resembles a gigantic ant-hill. More than ten thousand pilgrims, women as well as men, swarm up the steep and well-worn paths, sleep in rude huts, and in the early morning are the first of all their co-religionists to greet the Sun Goddess, Ama-Terasu, as with prayers and genuflections on the summit, they welcome the coming orb of day. It is said that the earth and ashes brought down by pilgrims' feet reascend spontaneously at night. It is now almost two centuries since Fuji's volcanic crater emitted its last fiery breath, and since that time it has slumbered peacefully, to all appearances wrapped in eternal sleep. But although the mountain is no longer a menace to the surrounding provinces, the same awful force that formerly found an outlet through its crater now manifests itself in frequent earthquake shocks; and happy is the town or village

Photograph by Enami

DEITIES

which has not at some time in its history been reduced to a
mere heap of débris.   Thus we begin to comprehend why the
Japanese are content with impermanency.   They are forced
by Providence to accept it.   As has been said, "The earthquakes condemn Japan to perpetual simplicity in building.
The very land revolts against the imposition of Western archi-
tecture, and occasionally even opposes the new course of
traffic by pushing railroad lines out of level or out of shape,"
or even by tumbling steel railway-bridges from their supports.
Nor do Japan's catastrophes come always in the form of earthquakes.   Sometimes an earthquake-wave, or so-called "tidal
wave," sweeps inland for an incredible distance, and then,
receding, carries houses, temples, human beings out to sea,

THE YAAMI HOTEL

— in an hour, a happy, prosperous shore is given to deso-
lation. This, we remember, is what occurred at Kamakura.

Sometimes the terror comes in still more awful form.
In 1888 a great volcano in the north, known as Bandaisan,
literally exploded. It devastated an area of twenty-seven
square miles. It leveled forests, turned rivers from their
courses, and buried villages with their entire population in a
flow of seething mud. Lafcadio Hearn tells us of a super-
stitious old peasant who watched the whole cataclysm from a
neighboring peak " as unconcernedly as if he had been looking at a drama. He saw a black column of ashes and steam
rise to the height of twenty thousand feet and spread out at
its summit in the shape of an umbrella, blotting out the sun ;
then he felt a strange rain pouring on him
hotter than the water of a bath, then all
became black, and he felt the mountain beneath him shaking to its roots
and heard a crash of thunders that
seemed like the sound of the break-
ing of a world ; but he remained

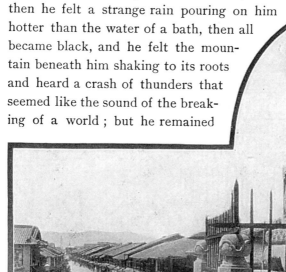

KYOTO

quite still until everything was over. He had made up his mind not to be afraid, deeming that all he saw and heard was delusion wrought by the witchcraft of a fox.''

Kyoto is the most attractive city of Japan. Formerly the residence of the reigning emperor, it is even now the

Photograph by Enami

THE GREAT BELL

stronghold of a proud conservatism that loves not the new
paths by which the nation is rushing headlong toward its new
ideals.　At Kyoto even the hotels dedicated to the comfort of
the foreigner are not unpicturesque, and the hotel Yaami bears
to a certain extent the imprint of its quaint surroundings.　It
stands on Maruyama, one of that historic range of hills that
like a verdured wall shuts in the Holy City.　On the slopes
a chain of gorgeous temples and monasteries rose during past
centuries, making of these hills a sort of sacred rampart,
crowned with the citadels of old religions ; and between two
of the most ancient monasteries the Yaami Inn stands forth,
its numerous verandas commanding a panorama of the plain
in which Kyoto lies.　The population
of the city is now much smaller
than in earlier years.　In 1868

Photograph by Enami

KIOMIZU

the Emperor removed his court to Tokyo, and since that time Kyoto has been shrinking, and many points of interest once well within the city are found at present in the open fields. In the flood-tide of its prosperity this capital found its broad and sheltered valley all too small, and so its sea of structures rolled slowly up the surrounding slopes. To-day that tide is at the ebb, only the temples having resisted the reflux, for they still cling proudly to their hillside groves; but as we stand here, thinking of Kyoto's lordly past, our reverie is rudely interrupted by a deafening boom, a sort of thunder-clap, made musical. And not a hundred yards away we find the source of this torrent of bronze music, for the deep waves of sound proceed from a huge bell, a dome of metal weighing almost a hundred tons. It has no metal tongue, but is made to speak by means of a huge beam of wood which, suspended horizontally from a scaffold, is swung, end on, against the brazen mass, send-ing out over the silent city a sonorous din of quivering brass. Not far from here we find the Kiomizu Temple, a place of worship high in favor with the poorer classes and unique in situation. It over-hangs a deep ravine and is supported by a scaffolding in which a veritable forest of big trees has been em-ployed.

We notice that just below the railing of the temple-terrace there is a

Photograph by O. M. Poole

A BAMBOO CORRIDOR

sort of picket-fence projecting at an angle of forty-five degrees. "What is it for?" we ask. "To keep the people from throwing rubbish into the ravine?" Not at all. It has been placed there by the government to curb the exuberant expressions of gratitude on the part of the ladies of the

Photograph by Otis A. Poole

TEA-PLANTS

congregation. Many a gentle little maid or wife having made secret vows to the gods has leaped from yonder terrace, not in disappointment, not in despair, but in pure thankfulness because the gods of Kiomizu had answered some tearful prayer or caused some blessing to descend upon the family of the suppliant, who thus freely offers her life in payment of a debt of gratitude. Strange, indeed, the Japanese idea of duty.

Continuing our ramble along this sacred slope we find ourselves suddenly in one of the delightful bamboo avenues that wind along Kyoto's guardian hills. Far above our heads the feathery tips are unceasingly in motion, swaying softly with the lightest breath, and, as they caress one another, making a gentle rustling sound that quite completes the charm. Lovely they are, but indispensable as well. We cannot picture a Japan without bamboo, for these same graceful trees are put to the most varied uses; their branches are twined into the very network of the manufactures of Japan. And then how rapidly they grow! To-day a little sprig — next week almost a tree.

A little farther on we pause before another Buddhist temple, and here let me remind you that it is to a priest of this religion that we owe the pleasures of the cup that cheers but not inebriates. For of the origin of the tea-plant the following legend is related: A certain Buddhist saint, renowned for rigorous living and long unbroken vigils, one night in spite of all his self-control fell fast asleep. On awakening he was so deeply chagrined to think that he had yielded to a human weakness that, in pious anger, he plucked out his eye-lashes and cast them on the ground. Then came the miracle. The lashes took root, and from

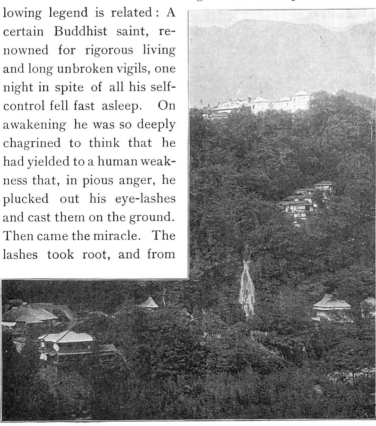

MIYANOSHITA

them sprouted a new, strange plant, the tea-plant, whose leaves have ever since possessed the power of keeping men awake all night. May blessings be upon that saint!

The temples of Kyoto seem almost numberless, and yet we found at the time of our visit two new temples rising from the heart of this long-since-completed city. Incredible, indeed, but true it is, that old wise Kyoto, not content with her three thousand half-deserted temples, must needs construct two more and make them grander, finer, and one of them more enormous, than any of the boasted structures of the past. What is more marvelous, the largest structure, the Higashi Hongwanji, rises, not with the aid of government or prince, as did the ancient shrines, but owes its being to the common people and the peasants, who, by gifts of money and material, of time and labor, have rendered possible this mighty undertaking. Clever carpenters have given their strength and skill to shape into pillars the gigantic trees that have

A MOUNTAIN OF CARPENTRY

been cut down and hauled to the city as offerings by worshipers whose homes are in far-distant forests. Those who had nothing to give yet gave something; witness the gigantic coils of rope, indeed the strangest offering of all, and the most pathetic, for, believe me, they are made of human hair. Yes, it is true — poor peasant women, destitute of all save their wealth of raven hair, sacrificed even their crowning glory, and, braiding their jet black tresses into mighty ropes, sent them to be employed in hauling timber for the construction of the temple. One of these cables is three hundred and sixty feet in length and nearly three inches in diameter. And now, the work accomplished, these coils of human hair remain as a memorial of the faith of unknown thousands of pious, gentle souls who have not hesitated to make sacrifice, at the call of duty, even of their good looks. And yet we have been told that Buddhism is a dying faith!

The Higashi Hongwanji cost no less than a full million dollars and was seventeen years in building. It is a hundred and twenty-seven feet in height, more than two hundred feet in length. It is a mountain of magnificent carpentry. There are beams forty-two feet long; pillars nine feet in circumference. The painting of the altar-screens cost ten thousand dollars, and the whole of this million-dollar structure has been paid for by the coppers of the poor. A

ROPES OF HUMAN HAIR

hundred thousand peasants came hither to attend the dedication. This looks as if the ancient Buddhist faith were very much alive in the hearts of the common people of Japan.

I could of course lead you on from temple to temple until the full three thousand have been visited, but I shall make your penance light and ask you to visit only one more—the famous Temple of the Thirty-three Thousand Gods. Here we may see at one glance more deities than we could see in a pilgrimage of forty days. The interior suggests a grand-stand at a Jubilee procession, filled with spectators from some strange Oriental paradise. A glittering company of heavenly beings is assembled here as if to witness some imposing ceremony; nor do we see them all. Behind us are massed an equal number of silent brazen figures, a host of Amazons, bristling with innumerable arms and weapons, their heads encircled by elaborate golden halos, their faces wreathed in that same supercilious Oriental smile—that smile with which the gods of the East look down upon terrestrial events.

RELIGIOUS MENDICANTS

Continuing our ramble through the streets, we pause to ask the meaning of a curious mound which occupies the center of a square. This, they inform us, is the "Mimi Zuka," and relate that in the good old days it was a custom for victorious generals to send home to the capital the heads of all the enemies slain in battle by their armies. The rival generals sent by Hideyoshi to conquer Korea, three hundred years ago, slew

Photograph by Enami

SOME OF THE THIRTY-THREE THOUSAND GODS

so many foes that their small fleets could not contain the heads ; so struck by a brilliant idea, they snipped off all the ears and noses of their slain adversaries, salted them carefully, and then shipped to Kyoto many a cargo of assorted Korean features, and these after being counted and their number recorded, were buried in this common grave. A tombstone was then raised in memory of this multitude of nasal and auricular appendages pertaining to the vanquished Sons of Cho-sen.

Leaving Kyoto, a delightful journey of one day by rikisha brings us to the site of Nara, another vanished capital of Old Japan. Nara was one of those famous metropolises that succeeded one another in the past. As has been said, no fewer than sixty cities have been in turn metropolis and capital. Most of them now have disappeared. A few, like Kamakura and Nara, survive as unimportant villages, because of their temples or their religious associations. Two of them only, Tokyo and Kyoto, rank among the living cities of to-day. A thousand years ago Nara was at the zenith of her prosperity and power. The sacred Emperor dwelt within her gates. Her streets were crowded with princes and pilgrims come to do homage and to worship there; but as to-day we wander through the famous temple groves of Nara, we meet only the tame deer that haunt the forest shades, and by their presence add to the impressive picturesqueness of the silent avenues. Nara was the cradle of Buddhism in Japan. Here the new faith brought by the priests from China was fostered by the sovereigns of the seventh and the eighth centuries. Here for the first time in Japan was preached the gospel of Gautama

THE MOUND OF THE KOREAN EARS

Buddha, the doctrine of salvation by self-perfectionment and meditation. The teachings of Buddha, spread broadcast over all the land, quickly won the hearts of men, and threatened the extinction of the native Shinto faith. The people enthusiastically embraced this new religion which taught that there was

Photograph by Enami   ONE OF THE NARA TEMPLES

no evil except the slavery to bodily desires and passions, and promised eternal peace to those who should by prayer and meditation attain the state of Buddhahood and be absorbed into the infinite soul of the universe, or, as it is expressed, enter Nirvana. But the Buddhist faith no longer reigns alone at Nara, for a Shinto temple occupies a place of honor in this grove, contrasting in its severe simplicity with the elaborateness of the earlier shrines. There is in the simple ritual of Shintoism, in the plainness and bareness of its temples, and in the absence of all idols—a dignity that charms us. The priests of Shinto, like the priests of Protestantism, are not debarred from matrimony. Many of them train their daughters to perform the sacred ''Kagura,'' a dance which dates from the mythical period and is one of the most solemn rites of the religion. On my arrival at the temple, a solitary visitor, I found the sacred dancers all arrayed in

THE SHINTO
CORYPHEES AT N

their immaculate robes, prepared to go through, at the pilgrim's

Photograph by Kimbei

KAGURA DANCERS

bidding, the slow, calm movements of the Kagura. I signify my willingness to pay the accustomed fee, and at my words, the priests don their ceremonial robes, an ancient dame brings forth a koto, and to an accompaniment of twanging strings and deep-drawn groans from the men, the dance itself begins. The sacred ballet-girls are scarcely more than fourteen years of age, but perform their task with a statue-like gravity ; they glide softly about, waving a sprig of green or a cluster of gilded bells. When the dance is done, they sink to the ground as if exhausted, and the monotonous chanting slowly dies away. It is at Nara also that we find the most hideous bronze Buddha of Japan. Though a seeming travesty of Kamakura's noble image, it is in reality much older and much larger ; but as a work of art this bronze is utterly beneath consideration. Its ugly head has been four times melted off by the burning of its temple ; and we cannot but regret the ill-advised generosity that has made possible the re-casting of so execrable a countenance.

AT NARA

Photograph by Kimbei

THE DAI BUTSU OF NARA

Our route is now westward to the famous Inland Sea. The Inland Sea is a calm expanse of imprisoned ocean, bounded by the great islands of Japan,—Hondo, Shikoku, and Kiushiu,—and dotted everywhere with innumerable tiny isles, usually bare and treeless, but of most fantastic shapes, and in the autumn sunsets glowing with rich shades of red and gold.

Every town, every little fishing-village, has its special charm; but everywhere the natives reply to our enthusiastic raptures, "Wait until you have seen Miyajima, the Sacred Island. Then may you praise the beauties of our land." And so it is with undisguised delight that we behold for the first time the summits of that much-reverenced isle; and our impatience to arrive increases as our coolies swiftly cover the intervening miles. As we approach, we note with pleasure that, unlike the other islands, Miyajima is not treeless and rocky, but buried in luxuriant verdure. To reach it we embark in a small boat and slowly cross the narrow strait that lies between the mainland and Miyajima. Soon our sampan

THE INLAND SEA

glides beneath a stately, wave-washed torii. The broad arms of the sacred gateway are extended as if to welcome the fisher pilgrims who come to pray at the temple—a temple that appears to float upon the surface of the bay. Beyond this torii everything is holy. In former days the faithful held the isle in such respect that dogs were not permitted to exist upon it; and, what is stranger still, no human being was permitted either to take up the burden of existence or to shuffle off this mortal coil upon its hallowed

A CURIOUS S
Photograph by Otis

shore. Nay, do not disbelieve me ; both births and

Photograph by Enami

THE TEMPLE OF MIYAJIMA

deaths were prohibited by the strict canons of the Buddhist
church. A traveler who should prove to be so inconsiderate
as to die at Miyajima would never be allowed to make a
second visit ; accordingly we solemnly resolve that as courtesy
demands it, we shall try to live at least until we reach some
other place, a place where we may die in peace without
offending the religious scruples of an entire population.

We do not wonder that the Japanese have sanctified the
island, for we know that to the Japanese everything that is
beautiful or strange is also holy. Even to us Miyajima
appears as a glorious out-of-door cathedral, with pinnacles
of rock for spires, maple-decked valleys for its aisles and

Photograph by Ogawa

THE TORII OF MIYAJIMA

chapels, great trees for pillars, the beauties of all nature for adornment, and for a dome, the eternal vault of blue. Every day of our stay reveals new beauties, and at last we enthusiastically agree that Miyajima merits well its title as one of the

FROM MY WINDOW AT MIYAJIMA

famous "San Kei" or "Three most lovely sights" in all Japan. Even the little tea-house where we make our home is more than commonly attractive. In it they say no foreigners have ever lodged before ; but I doubt not that the barbarous stranger is now a familiar figure in its dainty, matted rooms : that he has often pushed aside its paper windows and breathed the same sigh of delight as he looked down upon the village there below. Here is one of the most "real" corners of the Real Japan ; and when in December, 1892, I looked upon it, the thought that mine was the only foreign eye to feast on all this quaintness and this beauty gave me a sense of ownership in it all—the proud pagoda on the cliff—the modest dwellings far below—the granite stairways and the terraced streets,—of all these I took possession; and as I sat there in my tea-house window and looked out upon my realm of beauty, framed by the distant hazy mountains, encircled by the calm, blue waters of the Inland Sea, I was more proudly content with my possessions than were any of the old-time princes who surveyed rich subject-provinces from the upper gables of their feudal castles. But of all my

ON THE INLAND SEA

empire the scene my memory will last surrender,—the scene that is always first evoked by the mere mention of Japan, is that lovely vista from the pagoda on the promontory. From the tall cliff I looked upon the gorgeous sunsets of those short

December days, and lingering in the twilight watched the mysterious outline of the sacred Torii as it faded slowly into the gathering blackness of the night,—and the vanishment of that symbolic arch always reminded me that very soon my days in fair Japan would pass from the joyous light of the Present into the sober twilight of the Past; that it would soon be time for me to say a final "Sayonara"—a farewell. And how perfectly that musical word expresses what we feel in leaving fair Japan—for its literal meaning voices regret and gratitude. "Sayonara"—"if it must be so." But as I breathed the word, I found a consolation in the hope that as this scene was always conjured back by the dawning of the morrow's sun, so might the coming of some future morn bring to me on its golden wings the promise of another visit to Japan. Other richer journeys may await me, but none will have, for me the same peculiar charm, nor in remembrance give the same enthusiastic thrill; for the Japan that I have tried to show you and to tell you of, is the Japan that fascinated me when I was twenty-two.

FURTHER READING

The research division of the Library of Congress has published an excellent survey of Japan edited by Robert Worden, *Japan: A Country Study* (1992). See also the well-written guidebook issued by the Kodansha Publishing Co., *Japan: Profile of a Nation* (1995). A standard reference work is *The Cambridge Encyclopedia of Japan* (1993), by Richard Bowring and Peter Kornicki.

A lot has been written about the political and economic history of the Far East between 1875 and 1914. For a general overview of the subject, see the following three outstanding college-level textbooks: Kenneth Scott Latourette's *A Short History of the Far East*, Nathaniel Peffer's *The Far East*, and Harold M. Vinacke's *History of the Far East in Modern Times*.

—Dr. Fred L. Israel

CONTRIBUTORS

General Editor FRED L. ISRAEL is an award-winning historian. He received the Scribe's Award from the American Bar Association for his work on the Chelsea House series *The Justices of the United States Supreme Court.* A specialist in American history, he was general editor for Chelsea's *1897 Sears Roebuck Catalog.* Dr. Israel has also worked in association with Arthur M. Schlesinger, jr. on many projects, including *The History of U.S. Presidential Elections* and *The History of U.S. Political Parties.* He is senior consulting editor on the Chelsea House series *Looking into the Past: People, Places, and Customs,* which examines past traditions, customs, and cultures of various nations.

Senior Consulting Editor ARTHUR M. SCHLESINGER, JR. is the preeminent American historian of our time. He won the Pulitzer Prize for his book *The Age of Jackson* (1945), and again for *A Thousand Days* (1965). This chronicle of the Kennedy Administration also won a National Book Award. He has written many other books, including a multi-volume series, *The Age of Roosevelt.* Professor Schlesinger is the Albert Schweitzer Professor of Humanities at the City University of New York, and has been involved in several other Chelsea House projects, including the *American Statesmen* series of biographies on the most prominent figures of early American history.

IRVING WALLACE (1916-1990), whose essay on Burton Holmes is reprinted in the forward to The World 100 Years Ago, is one of the most widely read authors in the world. His books have sold over 200 million copies, and his best-sellers include *The Chapman Report, The Prize, The Man, The Word, The Second Lady,* and *The Miracle.*

INDEX

Artistry, 58-59
Asakusa, 37, 56, 59

Bamboo, 114-15
Bandaisan volcano, 110-11
Beauty, Japanese love of, 48, 53
Bowing, 74
Buddha, statues of, 86-87, 88-91, 123
Buddhism, 87-88, 118, 120-21

Cherry-trees, 38, 48-51
Children
  in festivals, 57-58
  as geisha, 62
Chrysanthemums, 54-55
Clothing, 72-74
Costumes, traditional Japanese, replaced by European dress, 72-74
Courtesy, 39, 70

Dai Butsu, 86-87, 88-91
Danjiro, 78
Deities
  in Temple of the Thirty-Three Thousand Gods, 118
  military chiefs as, 76
Drama, 78-79, 80-82

Earthquakes, 108-9
Earthquake-wave, 109-10

Eating, table-customs for, 42
Emperor of Japan
  European dress of, 73
  garden-party of, 55, 72
  palace of, 37, 71
Empress of Japan, European dress of, 72
Enoshima, 91
Entertainment, by geisha, 64, 67-68
European dress, traditional costumes replaced by, 72-74

Festivals, 57-58
Flower arranging, Japanese distaste for, 53-54
Foreigners
  perceived as angry, 70-71
  as travelers, 36-37, 39, 47
"Forty-seven Ronin, The," 76-78
Fuji-no-Yama, 47, 103-8
Fuji San. See Fuji-no-Yama
Furnishings, Japanese, 47-48
Futon, 48

Garden-party, of Mikado, 55, 72
Geisha, 40, 41, 60-68
Goddess of the Pic-

turesque, 99
God of Unripe Fruit, 98
Grief, Japanese expression of, 70
Hakoné Mountains, 94
Hakoné valleys, 103
Hara kiri, 76, 78, 79-80
Hearn, Lafcadio, writings of, on Japan, 83-86, 110-11
Hibachi, 48
Higashi Hongwanji, 116-18
Hospitality, 96-97
Housework, lack of, 94-95

Imperial Castle, 37, 71
Imperial Gardens, 55
Imperial Hotel, 36, 42
Inland Sea, 124, 129
Irises, 53

Jinrikisha. See Rikisha

Kago, for transportation, 100, 102-3
Kagura, 122-23
Kamakura, 86, 88-89, 110, 120, 123
Kiomizu Temple, 113-14
Kyoto, 83, 93, 111-20, 120

Lanterns
  as festival decorations, 58

in Shiba, 75-76

Maruyama, 112
Matsuri, 57-58
Mikado. *See* Emperor of
  Japan
Military chiefs, deifica-
  tion of, 76
Mimi Zuka, 119-20
Miyajima, 125-30
Miyanoshita, 94
Mukojima, 38

Nara, 120-23
Nature, Japanese love
  of, 53-54

Otomé Togé, 103, 104

Peasants, 95-96, 117, 118
Picnics, 59, 60
Pilgrims, to Fuji-no-
  Yama, 107-8
Plays, 78-79, 80-82
Prince Ako, in "The
  Forty-seven Ronin,"
  76, 77, 79

Rice, threshing of, 95-96
Rikisha, 37, 59, 69

Saké, 64, 67
Shiba, 75
Shintoism, 121-123
Shoes, as votive-offering,
  99-100
Shoguns, burial-place of,
  75
Sitting, Japanese-style,
  40-41, 81
Street-cars, 59
Streets, 68-69
Sumida River, 37, 48

Tatami, 47
Tea-houses, 53, 60-61,
  96, 128
Tea-plant, legend of,
  115-16
Temple of the Mercy
  Goddess, Kwannon,
  56
Temple of the Thirty-
  three Thousand
  Gods, 118
Temples
  of Asakusa, 56
  of Kyoto, 112, 113-14,
  115, 116-18
  of Nara, 120, 121, 122
  worship in, 99

Theater, 78-79, 80-82
Tidal wave, 109-10
Tokaido ("Highway of
  the Eastern Sea"), 91,
  93-94
Tokonoma, 47
Tokugawa family, tombs
  of, 75, 76
Tokyo, 36-37, 42, 56, 59,
  83, 93, 113, 120
Torii, of Miyajima, 125-
  26, 130
Toro, 75
Transportation
  kago as, 100, 102-3
  rikisha as, 37, 59, 69
  street-cars as, 59

Uyeno Park, 59-60

Volcanoes, 108, 110

Wrestling, 82-83

Yao Matsu ("The Place
  of the Eight Hundred
  Pine-Trees"), 38-39,
  43, 44, 47